knitted animal cozies

35 woolly creatures to keep things safe and warm

fiona goble

CICO BOOKS
LONDON NEW YORK

Published in 2016 by CICO Books
An imprint of Ryland Peters & Small Ltd
20–21 Jockey's Fields, London WC1R 4BW
341 E 116th St, New York, NY 10029

www.rylandpeters.com

10 9 8 7 6 5 4 3 2 1

Text © Fiona Goble 2016
Design, illustration, and photography
© CICO Books 2016

A CIP catalog record for this book is
available from the Library of Congress
and the British Library.

ISBN: 978 1 78249 369 3

Printed in China

Editor: Kate Haxell
Designer: Alison Fenton
Photographer: Penny Wincer
Stylist: Nel Haynes

Art director: Sally Powell
Production controller: Mai-Ling Collyer
Publishing manager: Penny Craig
Publisher: Cindy Richards

contents

introduction

Welcome to the world of knitted animal cozies, giving you the opportunity to create a warm and safe place for life's essentials, such as your phone, keys, book, tablet, and earphones. There are plenty of patterns for non-essential but nice-to-have items too—cozies for your hot water bottle, breakfast boiled egg, golf clubs, and even your favorite house plant.

Whether you're after a country look, like an adorable hedgehog to keep your teapot warm, or something more quirky such as a meerkat to keep your e-reader safe, this book has a woolly creature that will not only guard your possessions but make sure they look good, too.

I've divided the projects into four chapters, in which you can find items to enhance your kitchen, home, bag, and desk. Each pattern gives the skill level required: one star is for novice knitters, two stars for intermediate, and three-star patterns require more advanced skills, but most of the patterns are well within the grasp of "advanced beginner" knitters, and there's nothing too tricky.

There's also a good selection of smaller projects such as egg cozies and phone cozies that you can whip up in an evening or two, and which don't require much yarn. There are ideas for girls and boys, ladies and gents… and even a cute little bear cub cozy to hold a new baby. Many of the projects also make great gifts.

If you're just starting out, I suggest you begin with something really small and simple like our rabbit egg cozy. Once you've got that sussed, you could venture into something a little larger that requires more piecing together; these projects include the tea cozies and hot water bottle cozies. With a bit of practice and confidence under your belt, I'm sure you'll then feel ready to tackle one of the slightly more advanced patterns, such as the 1950s-style flamingo bottle cozy or the salamander pencil case, which is my personal favorite.

Before splashing out on yarn, please read through the pattern to make sure you know the techniques involved. I've given precise details of all the yarns I've used in each project. While you don't have to follow my choice exactly, if you use a different brand please make sure that it's the same thickness and that you buy a sufficient amount. And don't forget to knit a gauge (tension) square before you begin to check that your project will be the right size.

I'd love to see pictures of any items you make, so please contact me via my blog at fionagoble. wordpress.com. My blog is also the place where I post any pattern errata and tutorials on tricky bits, and can answer any queries.

I've had enormous fun developing these animal cozy patterns and I hope you enjoy creating your own versions every bit as much.

Fiona Goble

chapter 1

in the kitchen

baby owl
tea cozy

Owls may not immediately spring to mind when you think of a traditional brew, but I've fallen slightly head-over-heels with all things woodland and thought this chubby little fellow would make the perfect companion for my round teapot. The body is knitted in a super-thick yarn so it grows really quickly—and I promise the eyes are much simpler to knit than you probably think. Add a beak and a couple of button eye centers and you're done.

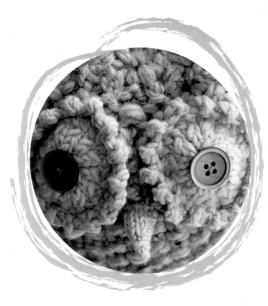

Yarn and materials

Lion Brand Wool-Ease Thick & Quick (83% acrylic, 10% wool, 8% rayon) super-bulky (super-chunky) yarn
    1 x 6oz (170g) ball (106yd/97m) in shade 154 Grey Marble (A)

Debbie Bliss Rialto DK (100% wool) light worsted (DK) yarn
    1 x 1¾oz (50g) ball (115yd/105m) in each of shades 044 Aqua (B) and 042 Pink (C)

Small amount of light worsted (DK) soft yellow yarn (D)

2 x ¾in (20mm) gray buttons

Gray sewing thread

Small amount of 100% polyester toy filling

Needles and equipment

US 11 (8mm) knitting needles

US 6 (4mm) knitting needles

US 3 (3.25mm) knitting needles

Yarn sewing needle

Standard sewing needle

Gauge (tension)
10 sts and 14 rows in stockinette (stocking) stitch to a 4-in (10-cm) square on US 11 (8mm) needles, using A.

Measurements
The finished cozy is 6in (15cm) tall excluding ear tufts and will fit a 5-cup round teapot.

Abbreviations
See page 126.

Skill level
★ ✩ ✩

To make cozy

Body
(Make 2)
Using US 11 (8mm) needles, cast on 21 sts in A.
Row 1: [K1, p1] to end, k1.
Rep row 1, 23 times more.

Row 25: [Sk2po, sl1 pwise, p2tog, psso] to last 3 sts, sk2po. *(7 sts)*
Row 26: [K1, p1] to last st, k1.
Row 27: P2tog, k1, p1, k1, p2tog. *(5 sts)*
Break yarn, thread through rem sts, and pull up securely.

Wings

(Make 2)

Using US 11 (8mm) needles, cast on 5 sts in A.

Row 1: [K1, p1] twice, k1.

Rep row 1, 5 times more.

Row 7: P2tog, k1, p2tog. *(3 sts)*

Row 8: P1, k1, p1.

Row 9: Sk2po. *(1 st)*

Break yarn and fasten off.

Eye base

(Make 2)

Using US 6 (4mm) needles, cast on 28 sts using B doubled.

Row 1: Knit.

Row 2: [P2tog] to end. *(14 sts)*

Rep rows 1–2 once more. *(7 sts)*

Break yarn, thread through rem sts, and pull up securely.

Eye fringes

(Make 2)

Using US 6 (4mm) needles, cast on 3 sts using C doubled.

*Bind (cast) off 2 sts, transfer rem st from right-hand to left-hand needle without turning work. One picot made.

Cast on 2 sts.*

Rep from * to * till you have 15 picots.

Fasten off.

Beak

Using US 3 (3.25mm) needles, cast on 10 sts in D.

Beg with a k row, work 2 rows st st.

Row 3: K1, ssk, k4, k2tog, k1. *(8 sts)*

Row 4: Purl.

Row 5: K1, ssk, k2, k2tog, k1. *(6 sts)*

Row 6: Purl.

Row 7: K1, ssk, k2tog, k1. *(4 sts)*

Row 8: [P2tog] twice. *(2 sts)*

Break yarn and thread through rem sts.

To make up

Thread one of the yarn tails at the top of one of the main cozy pieces though the rem sts of both pieces. Pull up tightly and secure. Using flat stitch (see page 125), sew up 1¾in (4.5cm) from the bottom and sew down 3in (7.5cm) from the top at the sides, to create holes for the handle and spout—or use your intended teapot as a guide.

Form eye bases into circles, join seam, and oversew (see page 125) in position. Oversew the eye fringes around the bases. Sew buttons in center using gray thread.

Sew beak seam, stuff lightly, and oversew in place.

For the ear tufts, cut two lengths of A, each measuring 56in (142cm). Secure the two ends under the spout for the tufts on the top of the head. Divide the big loop into four small loops and secure.

Weave in all loose ends.

According to the experts, sales of tea are booming. I thought I'd celebrate the fact with a ladybugs-and-squash tea cozy, to help you keep your second helping at the perfect temperature while you're enjoying your first refreshing cuppa. The green squash base is really simple to make, and while the ladybugs are a bit more of a challenge, you could soon find that knitting them is more addictive than tea drinking.

ladybug tea cozy

Yarn and materials

Patons Merino Extrafine Big (100% wool) bulky (chunky) yarn
    2 x 1¾oz (50g) balls (43yd/40m) in shade
    00373 Apple Green (A)

Debbie Bliss Rialto DK (100% wool) light worsted (DK) yarn
    1 x 1¾oz (50g) ball (115yd/105m) in shade
    012 Scarlet (B)

Sirdar Country Style DK (40% nylon, 30% wool 30% acrylic) light worsted (DK) yarn
    1 x 1¾oz (50g) ball (170yd/155m) in each of
    shade 610 Village Green (C) and 417 Black (D)

Small oddment of mid-gray light worsted (DK) yarn

Small oddment of black fingering weight (4-ply) cotton yarn

A handful of 100% polyester toy filling

Needles and equipment

US 10 (6 mm) knitting needles

US 3 (3.25mm) knitting needles

Yarn sewing needle

Large-eyed embroidery needle

Gauge (tension)

13 sts and 19 rows in stockinette (stocking) stitch to a 4-in (10-cm) square on US 10 (6 mm) needles, using A.

Measurements

The finished cozy is 7½in (19cm) tall excluding the stalk, and will fit a 5-cup round or slightly oval-shape teapot.

The ladybugs are 1½in (4cm) long.

Abbreviations

See page 126.

Skill level

★★☆

To make cozy

Squash

(Make 2)

Using US 10 (6mm) needles, cast on 29 sts in A.

Row 1: [K2, p2] to last st, k1.

Rep row 1, 31 times more.

Row 33: K2, [p3tog, k1] to last 3 sts, p2, k1. *(17 sts)*

Row 34: K2, p2, [k1, p1] to last st, k1.

Row 35: K1, [ssk] to last 2 sts, k2tog. *(9 sts)*

Row 36: [K1, p1] to last st, k1.

Row 37: [K2tog] to last st, k1. *(5 sts)*

Break yarn and thread through rem sts.

Stalk

Using US 3 (3.25mm) needles, cast on 6 sts in C.

Beg with a k row, work 14 rows in st st.

Bind (cast) off.

Leaves

(Make 2)

Using US 3 (3.25mm) needles, cast on 2 sts in C.

Row 1: [Inc] twice. *(4 sts)*

Row 2: Purl.

Row 3: K1, m1, k to last st, m1, k1. *(6 sts)*

Row 4: Purl.

Rep rows 3–4, 3 times more. *(12 sts)*

Beg with a k row, work 4 rows in st st.

Row 15: K1, k2tog, k to last 3 sts, ssk, k1. *(10 sts)*

Row 16: Purl.

Rep rows 15–16, 3 times more. *(4 sts)*

Row 23: K2tog, ssk. *(2 sts)*

Row 24: P2tog. *(1 st)*

Break yarn and fasten off.

Ladybugs

(Make 5)

Top

Using US 3 (3.25mm) needles, cast on 4 sts in B.

Row 1: [Inc, k1] twice. *(6 sts)*

Row 2: Purl.

Row 3: K1, m1, k4, m1, k1. *(8 sts)*

Work 5 rows in st st, beg with a p row.

Row 9: K1, ssk, k2, k2tog, k1. *(6 sts)*

Row 10: Purl.

Break B and join in D.

Work 2 rows in st st, beg with a k row.
Row 13: K1, ssk, k2tog, k1. *(4 sts)*
Break yarn and thread through rem sts.

Base

Using US 3 (3.25mm) needles, cast on 4 sts in D.
Row 1: [Inc, k1] twice. *(6 sts)*
Work 9 rows in st st, beg with a p row.
Row 11: K1, ssk, k2tog, k1. *(4 sts)*
Break yarn and thread through rem sts.

To make up

Place a top and base ladybug piece right sides together and oversew (see page 125) round the edges leaving a gap in the sides for turning and stuffing. Turn the right way out and stuff, then sew gap closed.

Using D, embroider a straight stitch (see page 123) for the dividing line between the wings and work French knots (see page 124) for the spots.

Using a separated strand of mid-gray light worsted yarn, work French knots for the eyes.

Thread a short length of the black cotton yarn in and out of the ladybug's head to form the antennae. Knot the ends and trim.

Thread one of the yarn tails at the top of one of the main cozy pieces though the rem sts of both pieces. Pull up tightly and secure. Using flat stitch (see page 124), sew up 1¾in (4.5cm) from the bottom and sew down 3in (7.5cm) from the top at the sides, to create holes for the handle and spout—or use your intended teapot as a guide.

Sew the leaves and stalk to the top of the cozy using C.

Sew the ladybugs onto the cozy using D and big straight stitches to form the ladybugs' legs.

Weave in all loose ends.

hen egg cozies

Admittedly the scale is not quite perfect—but what better way to keep your egg warm than to have a tweedy little hen sitting on it for you? I thought this tweed yarn would be perfect for knitting hens as soon as I saw it—and I've knitted it extra tightly so the cozy really will keep your eggs at the perfect temperature while you're sorting out a few urgent tasks before sitting down to eat.

Yarn

To knit both cozies

Sublime Luxurious Tweed DK light worsted (DK) yarn
1 x 1¾oz (50g) ball (148yd/135m) in each of shade 420 Dusk (A) and shade 394 Rich Amber (B)

Oddments of red and yellow light worsted (DK) yarns for combs and beaks

Small oddments of off-white and black light worsted (DK) yarns

Needles and equipment

US 7 (4.5mm) knitting needles

US 3 (3.25mm) knitting needles

Yarn sewing needle

Large-eyed embroidery needle

Gauge (tension)

16 sts and 27 rows in stockinette (stocking) stitch to a 4-in (10-cm) square on US 7 (4.5mm) needles, using yarn doubled.

Measurements

The finished cozies are 4in (10cm) wide at the widest point, and 3½in (9.5cm) tall to top of comb, and will fit a standard-size egg and egg cup.

Abbreviations

See page 126.

Skill level

★★☆

To make cozy

Side 1

Using US 7 (4.5mm) needles, cast on 14 sts in either A or B (as required) doubled.

Knit 2 rows.

Row 3: Purl.

Row 4 (RS): Inc, k to last 2 sts, inc, k1. *(16 sts)*

Row 5: Purl.

Row 6: K2, m1, k to last 2 sts, m1, k2. *(18 sts)*

Beg with a p row, work 7 rows in st st.*

Row 14: K9, bind (cast) off 4 sts, k to end.

Cont working on 5 sts just worked only, leaving rem sts on needle.

Next row: Purl.

Next row: Ssk, then using resulting st bind (cast) off to end. *(1 st)*

Break yarn and fasten off.

Rejoin yarn to rem sts on WS of work.

Next row: P2tog, p to end. *(8 sts)*

Next row: K to last 2 sts, k2tog. *(7 sts)*

Beg with a p row, work 3 rows in st st.

Next row: Ssk, k3, k2tog. *(5 sts)*

Next row: Purl.

Next row: Ssk, k1, k2tog. *(3 sts)*

Next row: P3tog. *(1 st)*

Break yarn and fasten off.

Side 2

Work as for side 1 to *.

Row 14: K5, bind (cast) off 4 sts, k to end.

Cont working on 9 sts just worked only, leaving rem sts on needle.

Next row: P to last 2 sts, p2tog. *(8 sts)*

Next row: Ssk, k to end. *(7 sts)*

Beg with a p row, work 3 rows in st st.

Next row: Ssk, k3, k2tog. *(5 sts)*

Next row: Purl.

Next row: Ssk, k1, k2tog. *(3 sts)*

Next row: P3tog. *(1 st)*

Break yarn and fasten off.

Transfer 5 sts to second needle and join yarn to rem sts on WS of work.

Next row: Purl.

Next row: Bind (cast) off 2 sts, k2tog, pass 2nd st on right-hand needle over last. *(1 st)*

Break yarn and fasten off.

Comb

Using US 3 (3.25mm) needles, cast on 4 sts in red light worsted (DK) yarn.

*Bind (cast) off 3 sts, transfer rem st from right-hand to left-hand needle without turning work.

Cast on 3 sts.*

Rep from * to * once more.

Bind (cast) off all sts.

Beak

Using US 3 (3.25mm) needles, cast on 6 sts in yellow light worsted (DK) yarn.

Bind (cast) off.

Making up

Embroider the wings in chain stitch (see page 123) using contrasting yarn—B on the cozy knitted in A, and A on the cozy knitted in B.

Using black light worsted (DK) yarn, work a French knot for the eye centers (see page 124) and using off-white light worsted (DK) yarn, work a ring of chain stitch around the French knots.

Place the two cozy pieces right sides together and oversew (see page 125) round the edges, leaving the base open. Turn the right way out.

Oversew the combs in place using yarn tails.

Fold the beak in half and stitch it in place along this fold using the yarn tails.

Weave in all loose ends.

If you're on the hunt for an egg cozy with a difference, you've arrived on the right page. This is a cozy that will not only look imperious, but will also keep your boiled eggs warm. I've knitted a male moose with a handsome pair of antlers—but you could knit a female relative for him as well if you want to, simply by omitting the antlers and adding a more girly bow.

moose egg cozy

Yarn and materials

King Cole Merino Blend DK (100% pure new wool) light worsted (DK) yarn
  1 x 1¾oz (50g) ball (113yd/104m) in each of shade 1764 Mink (A) and 41 Oatmeal (B)

Oddment of black light worsted (DK) yarn

2 x ⅜in (8mm) black dome buttons

Handful of 100% polyester toy filling

Black sewing thread

A 10-in (25-cm) length of ⅜-in (1-cm) wide red gingham ribbon

Needles and equipment

US 3 (3.25mm) knitting needles

Yarn sewing needle

Large-eyed embroidery needle

Standard sewing needle

Gauge (tension)

24 sts and 32 rows in stockinette (stocking) stitch to a 4-in (10-cm) square on US 3 (3.25mm) needles.

Measurements

The cozy is 3in (7.5cm) tall, excluding ears and antlers, and the circumference at the base is 6¾in (17cm).

Abbreviations

See page 126.

Skill level

★ ☆ ☆

To make cozy

Main head
Cast on 42 sts in A.
Row 1: Knit.
Beg with a k row, work 18 rows in st st.
Row 20: K2, [sl2, k1, p2sso, k4] 5 times, sl2, k1, p2sso, k2. (30 sts)
Row 21: Purl.
Row 22: K1, [sl2, k1, p2sso, k2] 5 times, sl2, k1, p2sso, k1. (18 sts)
Row 23: Purl.
Row 24: [Sl2, k1, p2sso] to end. (6 sts)
Break yarn, thread through rem sts and pull securely.

Nose
Cast on 16 sts in A.
Beg with a k row, work 4 rows in st st.
Break A and join in B.
Beg with a k row, work 2 rows in st st.
Row 7: [K2tog] to end. (8 sts)
Row 8: [P2tog] to end. (4 sts)
Break yarn, thread through rem sts, pull firmly, and secure.

Ear

(Make 2)
Cast on 5 sts in A.
Beg with a k row, work 6 rows in
st st.
Row 7: Ssk, k1, k2tog. *(3 sts)*
Row 8: P3tog. *(1 st)*
Break yarn and fasten off.

Antlers

(Make 4)
Cast on 12 sts in B.
*Bind (cast) off 4 sts. Transfer st
rem from binding (casting) off from
right-hand to left-hand needle
without turning work.
Cast on 2 sts.*
Rep from * to * 3 times more.
Bind (cast) off rem sts.

To make up

Sew the back seam of the cozy
using mattress stitch (see page 124).

Sew the nose seam using mattress
stitch. Stuff lightly and oversew (see
page 125) the nose in place on the
front of the cozy.

Sew on the button eyes using
needle and sewing thread.

With right sides facing, oversew
the two cast-on edges of two antler
pieces together. Do the same for
the other two pieces. Sew the
ears and antlers in place using the
photograph as a guide.

In black yarn, embroider two
French knots (see page 124) for the
nostrils and two straight stitches
(see page 123), one over the other,
for the mouth.

Tie the ribbon in a bow and secure
just under the nose.

Weave in all loose ends.

Why would you want to knit a plain old tea cozy when you can whip up a tea cozy mouse instead? I promise it won't make you scream and shout, munch its way through the breakfast cereal—or leave behind any unpleasant telltale signs. I've knitted this cozy in a beautiful pale gray with just a hint of pink, but you can make your mouse dark gray, black, white, or brown—or any fantasy mouse color you love.

mouse tea cozy

Yarn and materials

Debbie Bliss Cashmerino Aran (55% wool, 33% acrylic, 12% cashmere) worsted (Aran) yarn

  1 x 1¾oz (50g) ball (98yd/90m) in shade 027 Stone (A)

Small amount of pale pink light worsted (DK) yarn (B)

2 x ⅜in (8mm) black dome buttons

A handful of 100% polyester toy filling

Black sewing thread

Needles and equipment

US 7 (4.5mm) knitting needles

Yarn sewing needle

Standard sewing needle

Gauge (tension)

20 sts and 27 rows in stockinette (stocking) stitch to a 4-in (10-cm) square on US 7 (4.5mm) needles, using A.

Measurements

The cozy will fit a 2-cup teapot that is 4.5in (11cm) tall. The actual cozy is 4¼in (10.5cm) tall and has a circumference of 9½in (24cm).

Abbreviations

See page 126.

Skill level

★★☆

To make cozy

Main piece

(Make 2)

Cast on 24 sts in A.

Row 1: Knit.

Beg with a k row, work 4 rows in st st.

Row 6: K2, [m1, k4] 5 times, m1, k2. *(30 sts)*

Beg with a p row, work 21 rows in st st.

Row 28: K1, [sl2, k1, p2sso, k2] 5 times, sl2, k1, p2sso, k1. *(18 sts)*

Row 29: Purl.

Row 30: [Sl2, k1, p2sso] to end. *(6 sts)*

Break yarn, thread through rem sts, pull firmly, and secure.

Head

Cast on 34 sts in A.

Beg with a k row, work 2 rows in st st.

Row 3: K6, ssk, k1, k2tog, k12, ssk, k1, k2tog, k6. *(30 sts)*

Row 4 and every alt row: Purl.

Row 5: K5, ssk, k1, k2tog, k10, ssk, k1, k2tog, k5. *(26 sts)*

Row 7: K4, ssk, k1, k2tog, k8, ssk, k1, k2tog, k4. *(22 sts)*

Row 9: K3, ssk, k1, k2tog, k6, ssk, k1, k2tog, k3. *(18 sts)*

Row 11: K2, ssk, k1, k2tog, k4, ssk, k1, k2tog, k2. *(14 sts)*

Row 13: K1, ssk, k1, k2tog, k2, ssk, k1, k2tog, k1. *(10 sts)*

Row 15: Ssk, k1, k2tog, ssk, k1, k2tog. *(6 sts)*

Do not work a purl row after row 15.

Break yarn, thread through rem sts, pull firmly, and secure.

Ear

(Make 2)

Cast on 3 sts in A.

Row 1: [Inc] 3 times. *(6 sts)*

Beg with a p row, work 3 rows in st st.

Row 5: K1, ssk, k2tog, k1. *(4 sts)*

Row 6: [P2tog] twice. *(2 sts)*

Row 7: [Inc] twice. *(4 sts)*

Row 8: [Inc pwise, p1] twice. *(6 sts)*

Beg with a k row, work 3 rows in st st.

Row 12: [P2tog] 3 times. *(3 sts)*

Bind (cast) off.

Tail

Cast on 5 sts in B.

Beg with a k row, work 60 rows in st st.

Row 61: Ssk, k1, k2tog. *(3 sts)*

Break yarn, thread through rem sts, pull firmly, and secure.

To make up

Thread one of the yarn tails at the top of one of the main cozy pieces though the rem sts of both pieces. Pull up tightly and secure. Sew down 2½in (6cm) at the top of both sides with flat stitch (see page 125) and sew up ½in (1.5cm) at the bottom of both sides, so that you leave a space for the handle and spout.

Sew the lower seam of the head using mattress stitch (see pages 124–125), stuff, then sew the eyes in place. Oversew (see page 125) the head in position.

Fold the ear pieces so the right sides are on the inside and oversew the curved edges, leaving the lower edge open. Turn the right way out and sew in place using the photograph as a guide.

Using B, work a coil of chain stitches (see page 123) for the nose.

Join the long seam of the tail and stitch in place.

Weave in all loose ends.

sheep cafetière hug

Thick and extremely woolly, this cozy will definitely keep your coffee warm long enough for you to enjoy a second cup—and will also make your coffee pot look a lot cuter. The cozy is knitted on big needles, so will come together quickly, and adding the face and topknot is much easier than it looks. So if you're looking for the perfect gift for coffee-loving friends, you can stop right here.

Yarn and materials

Lion Brand Wool-Ease Thick & Quick (83% acrylic, 10% wool, 8% rayon) super-bulky (super-chunky) yarn

   1 x 6oz (170g) ball (106yd/97m) in shade 099 Fisherman (A)

Small amount of dark gray light worsted (DK) yarn (B)

2 x ⅜in (8mm) black dome buttons

Oddment of black light worsted (DK) yarn

Small amount of 100% polyester toy filling

A 2½-in (6-cm) strip of sew-in white hook-and-loop (Velcro) tape

Black and white sewing thread

Needles and equipment

Size US 10 (6mm) knitting needles

Size US 3 (3.25mm) knitting needles

Yarn sewing needle

Large-eyed embroidery needle

Standard sewing needle

Gauge (tension)

13 sts and 16 rows in stockinette (stocking) stitch to a 4-in (10-cm) square on US 10 (6mm) needles using A.

Measurements

The cozy is 5½in (14cm) across and 4½in (11cm) tall and will fit a pot that is approximately 6in (15cm) tall and 3½in (9cm) in diameter.

Abbreviations

See page 126.

Skill level

★★☆

To make cozy

Body
Using US 10 (6mm) needles, cast on 32 sts in A.
Row 1: [K1, p1] to end.
Row 2: [P1, k1] to end.
Rep rows 1–2 once more.
Row 5: Cast on 4 sts, [k1, p1] to end. *(36 sts)*
Row 6: [P1, k1] to end.
Row 7: [K1, p1] to end.
Row 8: [P1, k1] to end.
Rep rows 7–8, 4 times more.
Row 17: Bind (cast) off 4 sts, [p1, k1] to last st, p1.
(32 sts)
Row 18: [P1, k1] to end.
Row 19: [K1, p1] to end.
Row 20: [P1, k1] to end.
Rep rows 19–20 once more.
Bind (cast) off.

Head
Using US 3 (3.25mm) needles, cast on 16 sts in B.
Beg with a k row, work 8 rows in st st.
Row 9: K2tog, k to last 2 sts, ssk. *(14 sts)*
Beg with a p row, work 5 rows in st st.
Row 15: K2tog, k to last 2 sts, ssk. *(12 sts)*
Row 16: Purl.
Rep rows 15–16 once more. *(10 sts)*
Row 19: K2tog, k to last 2 sts, ssk. *(8 sts)*
Row 20: P2tog, p to last 2 sts, p2tog. *(6 sts)*
Row 21: K2tog, k2, ssk. *(4 sts)*
Bind (cast) off pwise.

Ear
(Make 2)
Using US 3 (3.25mm) needles, cast on 3 sts in B.
Row 1: [Inc] twice, k1. *(5 sts)*
Beg with a p row, work 3 rows in st st.
Row 5: Ssk, k1, k2tog. *(3 sts)*
Row 6: Purl.
Row 7: Sk2po. *(1 st)*
Break yarn and fasten off.

Topknot
Using A, cast on 7 sts using US 10 (6mm) needles.
Bind (cast) off.

To make up

Join the two short edges by sewing using flat stitch (see page 125) ⅜in (1cm) at the top and bottom, leaving space for the handle.

Cut the piece of hook-and-loop (Velcro) tape in half lengthwise—you will only need one piece. Sew the hook part to the underside of the flap and the loop side in a corresponding position on the main cozy.

Sew the buttons for eyes onto the face and oversew (see page 125) the sides of the face in position on the main cozy. Stuff and stitch across the top.

Sew the ears and topknot in place.

Using the photograph as a guide, sew the nose in black using straight stitches (see page 123).

Weave in all loose ends.

rabbit egg cozies

As probably the easiest as well as the quickest project in the book, this is an ideal place to get started. Simply knitted in a combination of seed (moss) stitch and stockinette (stocking) stitch, these bunnies will come together very quickly.

Yarn

For blue cozy
Debbie Bliss Rialto Chunky (100% extra-fine merino) bulky (chunky) yarn
1 x 1¾oz (50g) ball (66yd/60m) in shade 010 Duck Egg

For pink cozy
Wendy Merino Chunky (100% pure merino wool) bulky (chunky) yarn
1 x 1¾oz (50g) ball (71yd/65m) in shade 2473 Rhubarb

Small amount of off-white bulky (chunky) yarn

Oddment of black light worsted (DK) yarn

Needles and equipment

US 9 (5.5mm) knitting needles

Yarn sewing needle

Large-eyed embroidery needle

Gauge (tension)

16 sts and 22 rows in stockinette (stocking) stitch to a 4-in (10-cm) square on US 9 (5.5mm) needles.

Measurements

The cozies are 3½in (9cm) tall and the circumference at the base is 7½in (19cm).

Abbreviations

See page 126.

Skill level

★ ✩ ✩

To make cozy

Main piece
Cast on 32 sts in main yarn.
Row 1: [K1, p1] to end.
Row 2: [P1, k1] to end.
Row 3: [K1, p1] to end.
Beg with a p row, work 15 rows in st st.
Row 19: K2, [sl2, k1, p2sso, k2] to end. *(20 sts)*
Row 20: P2tog, p to last 2 sts, p2tog. *(18 sts)*
Row 21: [Sl2, k1, p2sso] to end. *(6 sts)*
Break yarn, thread through rem sts, pull firmly, and secure.

Ear
(Make 2)
Cast on 4 sts.
Row 1: [K1, p1] twice.
Row 2: [P1, k1] twice.

Rep rows 1–2, 7 times more.
Row 17: P2tog, k2tog. *(2 sts)*
Row 18: K2tog. *(1 st)*
Break yarn and fasten off.

To make up

Sew the main seam of the cozy using mattress stitch (see page 124).

Sew the ears in place and stitch the two sides of the base of each ear together, to give them some shape.

Using black yarn, embroider two small coils of chain stitch (see page 123) for the eyes. Using the same yarn, work a cross stitch for the nose.

Using the off-white yarn, work a row of running stitch, just above the lower border, using the photograph as a guide.

Weave in all loose ends.

hedgehog tea cozy

Possibly the cutest of all woodland creatures, you can now transform this prickly little animal into a flea-free cozy to keep your favorite brew warm at teatime—or any other time of day.

Yarn and materials

Katia Air Alpaca (54% alpaca, 46% nylon) worsted (Aran) yarn
>   1 x 0.9oz (25g) ball (126yd/115m) in shade 203 Pale Brown (A)

Drops Nepal Mix (65% wool, 35% alpaca) worsted (Aran) yarn
>   1 x 1¾oz (50g) ball (82yd/75m) in shade 0206 Light Beige (B)

2 x black ⅜in (8mm) dome buttons

Oddment of black light worsted (DK) yarn

Black sewing thread

A handful of 100% polyester toy filling

Needles and equipment

US 7 (4.5mm) knitting needles

US 3 (3.25mm) knitting needles

Stitch holder

Yarn sewing needle

Large-eyed embroidery needle

Standard sewing needle

Gauge (tension)

18 sts and 22 rows in stockinette (stocking) stitch to a 4-in (10-cm) square on US 7 (4.5mm) needles, using A.

Measurements

The cozy will fit a 2-cup teapot that is 4.5in (11cm) tall. The actual cozy is 4½in (11cm) tall and has a circumference of 11in (28cm).

Abbreviations

See page 126.

Skill level

★★☆

To make cozy

Main piece

(Make 2)

Using US 7 (4.5mm) needles, cast on 30 sts in A.

Row 1: [K2, p2] to last 2 sts, k2.

Row 2: [P2, k2] to last 2 sts, p2.

Knit 2 rows.

Rep rows 1–4 (last 4 rows) 6 times more.

Row 29: [K2tog, p2] to last 2 sts, k2tog. *(22 sts)*

Row 30: [P1, k2] to last st, p1.

Row 31: [K1, k2tog] to last st, k1. *(15 sts)*

Row 32: Knit.

Row 33: K1, [k2tog] 3 times, k1, [k2tog] 3 times, k1. *(9 sts)*

Row 34: [K2tog] twice, k1, [k2tog] twice. *(5 sts)*

Break yarn, thread through rem sts, and leave sts on stitch holder.

Head

Using US 7 (4.5mm) needles, cast on 30 sts using A doubled.

Knit 2 rows.

Break A and join a single strand of B.

Row 3: K5, ssk, k1, k2tog, k10, ssk, k1, k2tog, k5. *(26 sts)*

Row 4 and every alt row unless stated: Purl.

Row 5: K4, ssk, k1, k2tog, k8, ssk, k1, k2tog, k4. *(22 sts)*

Row 7: K3, ssk, k1, k2tog, k6, ssk, k1, k2tog, k3. *(18 sts)*

Row 9: K2, ssk, k1, k2tog, k4, ssk, k1, k2tog, k2. *(14 sts)*

Row 11: K1, ssk, k1, k2tog, k2, ssk, k1, k2tog, k1. *(10 sts)*

Row 13: Ssk, k1, k2tog, ssk, k1, k2tog. *(6 sts)*

Do not work a purl row after row 13.

Break yarn and thread through rem sts.

Ear

(Make 2)

Separate a 12-in (30-cm) length of A so that one length contains one strand and one length contains two strands; the former can be discarded.

Using US 3 (3.25mm) needles and the 2-strand length, cast on 4 sts.

Row 1: Knit.

Row 2: Ssk, k2tog. *(2 sts)*

Row 3: K2tog. *(1 st)*

Break yarn and fasten off.

To make up

Thread one of the yarn tails at the top of one of the main cozy pieces though the rem sts of both pieces. Pull up tightly and secure.

Sew down 2½in (6cm) at the top of both sides using flat stitch (see page 125) and sew up ½in (1.5cm) at the bottom of both sides, so that you leave a space for the handle and spout.

Sew the lower seam of the head using mattress stitch (see pages 124–125), stuff, then sew the eyes in position. Oversew (see page 125) the head in place and sew on the ears using the photograph as a guide.

Using the black yarn, work a coil of chain stitches (see page 123) for the nose.

Weave in all loose ends.

Puffins are of the world's most striking-looking birds—and I thought their face would translate nicely into a cozy for those who'd like their eggs kept warm by a less traditional feathered friend. There's a bit of two-color knitting involved, but it's pretty straightforward so this is an ideal project for those who want to dip their toe into the world of intarsia knitting and take things a step at a time.

puffin egg cozy

Yarn and materials

Debbie Bliss Rialto Chunky (100% extra-fine merino) bulky (chunky) yarn
  1 x 1¾oz (50g) ball (66yd/60m) in each of shade 001 Black (A) and 003 Ecru (B)

Oddments of light worsted (DK) yarn in dark gray (C) and orange (D). I used Patons Merino Extrafine DK in shade 198 Charcoal Heather and Katia Merino DK in shade 020.

2 x ⅜in (8mm) black dome buttons

Needles and equipment

US 9 (5.5mm) knitting needles

Yarn sewing needle

Large-eyed embroidery needle

Gauge (tension)

16 sts and 22 rows in stockinette (stocking) stitch to a 4-in (10-cm) square on US 9 (5.5mm) needles using A or B.

Measurements

The cozy is 3½in (9cm) tall and the circumference at the base is 7½in (19cm).

Abbreviations

See page 126.

Skill level

★★★

To make cozy

Main piece

Before you start, cut off two lengths of A, each approx. 1yd (92cm) long.

Cast on 32 sts in A from main ball.

Row 1: Knit.

Beg with a k row, work 4 rows in st st.

Row 6 (place chart): K5 in A, join in B and k4, join in separate length of A and k14, join in B from center of ball and k4, join in A from center of ball and k to end. Work rows 2–4 of chart.

Break length of A and main length (on outside of ball) of B.

Work rem of chart, joining in second length of A in second group of black stitches and rejoining B from outside of ball on second group of cream stitches on row 8 of chart.

After row 11 of chart, break all yarns except leading A and complete remainder of cozy in A.

Row 17: Purl.

Row 18: K2, [sl2, k1, p2sso, k2] to end. *(20 sts)*

Row 19: P2tog, p to last 2 sts, p2tog. *(18 sts)*

Row 20: [Sl2, k1, p2sso] to end. *(6 sts)*

Break yarn, thread through rem sts, pull firmly, and secure.

Beak

(Make 2)

Use yarns C and D doubled throughout.

Cast on 9 sts in C.

Row 1: K1 in D, k7 in C, k1 in D.

Row 2: P2 in D, p5 in C, p2 in D.

Row 3: K3 in D, k3 in C, k3 in D.

Row 4: P4 in D, p1 in C, p4 in D.

Break C and work rem of beak in D only.

Row 5: Ssk, k to last 2 sts, k2tog. *(7 sts)*

Row 6: Purl.

Row 7: Ssk, k to last 2 sts, k2tog. *(5 sts)*

Row 8: P2tog, p1, p2tog. *(3 sts)*

Row 9: Sl2, k1, p2sso. *(1 st)*

Break yarn and fasten off.

To make up

Place the two beak pieces right sides together and oversew (see page 125) around the curved edges, leaving the cast-on edges unstitched. Turn the piece the right way out.

Sew the seam of the main cozy using mattress stitch (see pages 124–125), leaving a gap for the beak. Insert the beak and oversew in place on both sides.

Using a single strand of A, work a curve of chain stitch (see page 123) using the photograph as a guide.

Sew eyes in place.

Weave in all loose ends.

Puffin egg cozy chart   ■ A   □ B

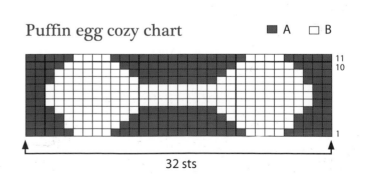

32 sts

chapter 2
at home

fox hot water bottle cozy

Could there be anything quite as lovely as a sleepy-faced fox to keep you warm on a cold winter evening? Well, I think it would be a hard act to follow—and this gorgeous boy would also make a super gift. The cozy is knitted in a stunning shade of rusty red yarn that, even though it has a dash of alpaca, is machine-washable and can even be tumble dried. Warm and fuzzy thoughts all round.

Yarn and materials

Wendy Serenity Chunky (70% acrylic, 20% alpaca, 10% wool) bulky (chunky) yarn

    1 x 3½oz (100g) ball (87yd/80m) in shade 3210 Auburn (A)

    1 x 3½oz (100g) ball (87yd/80m) in shade 3213 Cream (B)

Oddment of light worsted (DK) yarn in black

1 x ¾in (22mm) black button

1 x ½in (11mm) snap fastener

Needles and equipment

US 10 (6mm) knitting needles

Yarn sewing needle

Large-eyed embroidery needle

Gauge (tension)

15 sts and 18 rows in stockinette (stocking) stitch to a 4-in (10-cm) square on US 10 (6mm) needles.

Measurements

The finished cozy is 13in (33cm) long (excluding ears) when on the hot water bottle and will fit a standard hot water bottle measuring 12¾in (32.5cm) long (including neck) and 8in (20cm) wide.

Abbreviations

See page 126.

Skill level

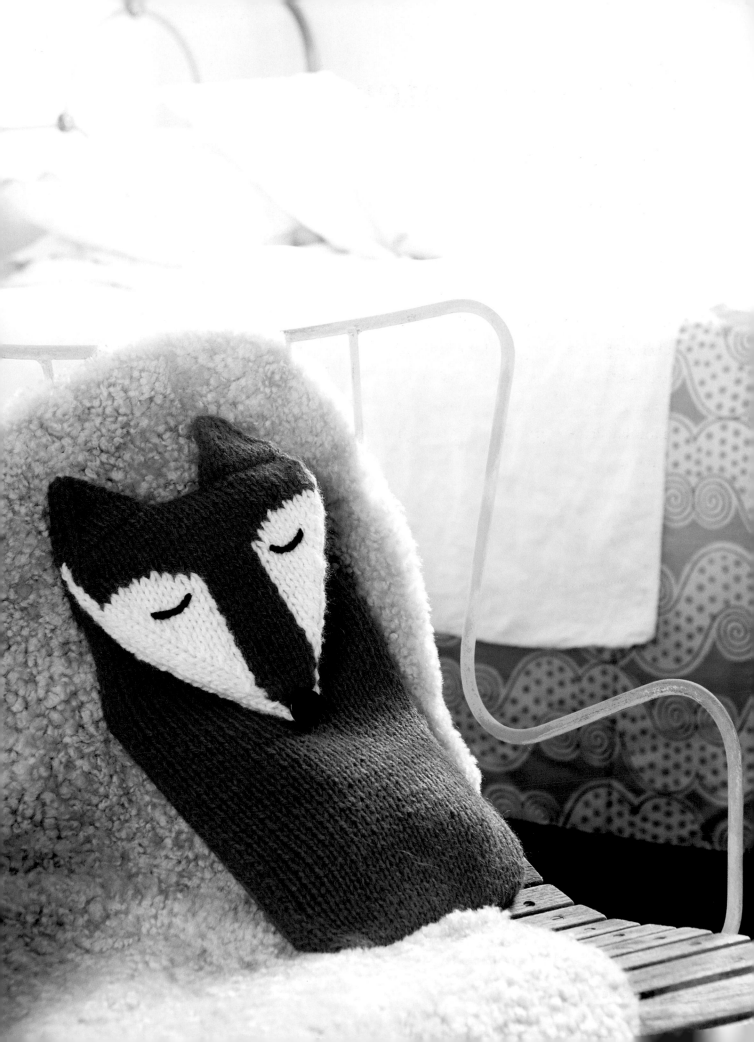

To make cozy

Front and back
(Make 2)

Cast on 28 sts in A.

Beg with a k row, work 54 rows in st st.

Knit 6 rows.

Bind (cast) off.

Face

Wind off a separate 5yd (5m) ball of A.

Cast on 28 sts in A from main ball.

Beg with a k row, work 6 rows in st st.

Row 7: K2, k2tog, k to last 4 sts, ssk, k2. *(26 sts)*

Row 8: Purl.

Row 9: Join in B and k5 in B using yarn from outside of ball, k16 in A from separate ball of A, k5 in B using yarn from center of ball.

Row 10: P7 in B, p12 in A, p7 in B.

Row 11: K8 in B, k10 in A, k8 in B.

Row 12: P9 in B, p8 in A, p9 in B.

Row 13: K2, k2tog, k6 in B, k6 in A, k6, ssk, k2 in B. *(24 sts)*

Row 14: P8 in B, p8 in A, p8 in B.

Row 15: K2, k2tog, k5 in B, k6 in A, k5, ssk, k2 in B. *(22 sts)*

Row 16: P8 in B, p6 in A, p8 in B.

Row 17: K2, k2tog, k4 in B, k6 in A, k4, ssk, k2 in B. *(20 sts)*

Row 18: P7 in B, p6 in A, p7 in B.

Row 19: K2, k2tog, k3 in B, k6 in A, k3, ssk, k2 in B. *(18 sts)*

Row 20: P6 in B, p6 in A, p6 in B.

Row 21: K2, k2tog, k2 in B, k6 in A, k2, ssk, k2 in B. *(16 sts)*

Row 22: P5 in B, p6 in A, p5 in B.

Row 23: K2, k2tog, k1 in B, k6 in A, k1, ssk, k2 in B. *(14 sts)*

Row 24: P4 in B, p6 in A, p4 in B.

Row 25: K2, k2tog in B, k6 in A, ssk, k2 in B. *(12 sts)*

Row 26: P3 in B, p6 in A, p3 in B.

Row 27: K2, k2tog in B, k4 in A, ssk, k2 in B. *(10 sts)*

Row 28: P3 in B, p4 in A, p3 in B.

Row 29: K1, k2tog in B, k4 in A, ssk, k1 in B. *(8 sts)*
Break both strands of B and work rest of piece in A only.

Row 30: Purl.

Row 31: [K2tog] twice, [ssk] twice. *(4 sts)*

Row 32: Purl.

Row 33: K2tog, ssk. *(2 sts)*

Row 34: P2tog. *(1 st)*
Break yarn and fasten off.

Head underside

Cast on 28 sts in B.

Beg with a k row, work 6 rows in st st.

Row 7: K2, k2tog, k to last 4 sts, ssk, k2. *(26 sts)*

Beg with a p row, work 5 rows in st st.

Row 13: K2, k2tog, k to last 4 sts, ssk, k2. *(24 sts)*

Row 14: Purl.

Rep rows 13–14, 8 times more. *(8 sts)*

Row 31: [K2tog] twice, [ssk] twice. *(4 sts)*

Row 32: Purl.

Row 33: K2tog, ssk. *(2 sts)*

Row 34: P2tog. *(1 st)*

Break yarn and fasten off.

Ear

(Make 2)

Cast on 12 sts in A.

Beg with a k row, work 2 rows in st st.

Row 3: K1, ssk, k6, k2tog, k1. *(10 sts)*

Row 4: Purl.

Row 5: K1, ssk, k4, k2tog, k1. *(8 sts)*

Row 6: Purl.

Row 7: K1, ssk, k2, k2tog, k1. *(6 sts)*

Row 8: Purl.

Row 9: K1, ssk, k2tog, k1. *(4 sts)*

Row 10: [P2tog] twice. *(2 sts)*

Row 11: K2tog. *(1 st)*

Row 12: Inc pwise. *(2 sts)*

Row 13: [Inc] twice. *(4 sts)*

Row 14: Purl.

Row 15: K1, m1, k2, m1, k1. *(6 sts)*

Row 16: Purl.

Row 17: K1, m1, k4, m1, k1. *(8 sts)*

Row 18: Purl.

Row 19: K1, m1, k6, m1, k1. *(10 sts)*

Row 20: Purl.

Row 21: K1, m1, k8, m1, k1. *(12 sts)*

Beg with a p row, work 2 rows in st st.

Bind (cast) off kwise.

To make up

Embroider the eyes in chain stitch (see page 123) using a separated strand of black yarn.

Place face and head underside pieces right sides together and oversew (see page 125) around the sides. Turn the head the right way out and join the top edges using mattress stitch (see page 125).

Fold the ear pieces so the right sides are together and oversew along sides leaving the lower edges open for turning. Turn the right way out, oversew along lower edge and stitch the ears in position.

Join side seams of main cozy in flat stitch (see page 125) and lower edges in mattress stitch. Oversew top of head to top edge of back of main cozy.

Sew button in place for the nose. Sew the top of the snap fastener under the button and the corresponding part on the front of the cozy.

Weave in all loose ends.

butterfly
vase cozy

If you want to customize your flower vase to complement your favorite blooms, look no further. This super-simple lace stitch knits up easily and will stretch over a barrel vase as well as one with straight sides. If you want a bigger cozy, simply cast on some extra stitches—making sure there's still an even number—and carry on knitting till your cozy is the right size.

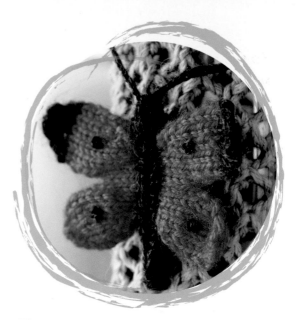

Yarn

Rowan Softknit Cotton (92% cotton, 8% polyester) light worsted (DK) yarn
    1 x 1¾oz (50g) ball (115yd/105m) in shade
    579 Dark Lime (A)

Small amounts of dark gray (B) and bright pink (C) light worsted (DK) wool or wool-mix yarns for butterflies

Needles and equipment

US 6 (4mm) knitting needles

US 3 (3.25mm) knitting needles

US C-2 (2.75mm) crochet hook—or one of similar size

Yarn sewing needle

Large-eyed embroidery needle

White (PVA) glue (optional)

Gauge (tension)

22 sts and 30 rows in stockinette (stocking) stitch to a 4-in (10-cm) square on US 6 (4mm) needles.

Measurements

The cozy is designed to fit a cylindrical vase that is 9¾in (25cm) tall and 2¾in (7cm) in diameter. It has considerable stretch though and you can always knit it a bit shorter or longer if you need to.

Abbreviations

See page 126.

Skill level

★★★

To make cozy

Main piece

Using US 6 (4mm) needles, cast on 34 sts in A.
Row 1: K1, [k2tog, yo] to last st, k1.
Row 2: Purl.
Row 3: K1, [yo, k2tog] to last st, k1.
Row 4: Purl.
Rep last 4 rows 15 times more.
Knit 3 rows.
Bind (cast) off.

Butterfly body

Using US 3 (3.25mm) needles, cast on 2 sts in B.
Row 1: [Inc] twice. *(4 sts)*
Row 2: Purl.
Row 3: K1, m1, k2, m1, k1. *(6 sts)*
Beg with a p row, work 15 rows in st st.
Row 19: Ssk, k2, k2tog. *(4 sts)*
Row 13: [P2tog] twice. *(2 sts)*
Break yarn and fasten off.

Butterfly antenna

Separate a 20-in (51-cm) length of B into two strands.
Using the crochet hook and one of the strands, make a
4¼-in (11-cm) chain (see page 121), pulling each loop
fairly tightly.

Butterfly wing side 1

Decide which is the head end and tail end of the
butterfly body.
Using US 3 (3.25mm) needles and starting from head
end and with RS facing, pick up and knit 8 sts in C
along one side of body.
Row 2: Inc pwise, p to last 2 sts, inc pwise, p1. *(10 sts)*
Row 3: Inc, k to last 2 sts, inc, k1. *(12 sts)*
Row 4: Purl.
Row 5: K1, m1, k to last st, m1, k1. *(14 sts)*
Row 6: Purl.
Row 7: K7, turn and work on these 7 sts only, leaving
rem sts on needle.*
Beg with a p row, work 3 rows in st st.
Break C and join in B.
Next row: Knit.
Next row: P2tog, p to last 2 sts, p2tog. *(5 sts)*
Next row: Ssk, k1, k2tog. *(3 sts)*
Next row: Purl.

Next row: Sk2po. *(1 st)*
Break yarn and fasten off.
With RS facing, rejoin C to rem sts.
Beg with a k row, work 3 rows in st st.
Next row: P2tog, p to last 2 sts, p2tog. *(5 sts)*
Next row: Ssk, k1, k2tog. *(3 sts)*
Next row: P3tog. *(1 st)*
Break yarn and fasten off.

Butterfly wing side 2

With RS facing, using US 3 (3.25mm) needles and
starting from tail end, pick up and knit 8 sts in C along
other side of body.
Work as for Side 1 to *.
Cont in C.
Beg with a p row, work 2 rows in st st.
Next row: P2tog, p to last 2 sts, p2tog. *(5 sts)*
Next row: Ssk, k1, k2tog. *(3 sts)*
Next row: P3tog. *(1 st)*
Break yarn and fasten off.
With RS facing, rejoin C to rem sts.
Beg with a k row, work 4 rows in st st.
Break C and join in B.
Next row: Knit.
Next row: P2tog, p to last 2 sts, p2tog. *(5 sts)*
Next row: Ssk, k1, k2tog. *(3 sts)*
Next row: Purl.
Next row: Sk2po. *(1 st)*
Break yarn and fasten off.

To make up

Sew up back seam of cozy using flat stitch (see page
125).

Thread antenna through the butterfly's head and trim
the yarn tails.

Using B, embroider a French knot (see page 124) on
the top of each front wing.

To make sure antennae stay straight, once they are in
place, soak them in a solution of one part white (PVA)
glue to nine parts water, stretch them out, and let dry.

Sew butterfly in place using photo as a guide.

Weave in all loose ends.

This delightful outfit will keep the baby in your life warm and cozy, as well as making sure that the new arrival looks almost unbelievably cute. I've knitted it in a beautiful soft yarn that comes in a wide range of colors, contains wool for warmth, and can be popped in the washing machine when it needs refreshing. The outfit is designed for babies from birth to three months, and I reckon it would make a much-appreciated gift for new parents.

bear cub
baby cocoon and hat

Yarn

Cascade Pacific Chunky (60% acrylic, 40% wool) bulky (chunky) yarn
  2 x 3½oz (100g) balls (120yd/110m) in shade 15 Taupe

(If you are knitting the cocoon only, you will still use more than one ball. If you are knitting the hat only, one ball will be plenty)

Needles and equipment

US 10½ (6.5mm) knitting needles
US 10 (6mm) knitting needles
Yarn sewing needle

Gauge (tension)

14 sts and 17 rows in stockinette (stocking) stitch to a 4-in (10-cm) square on US 10 (6.5mm) needles.

Measurements

The cocoon is 16½in (42cm) long from the top edge to the knot and the hat is 12in (30cm) in circumference. Both items will fit an average-size baby from birth to three months. For safety reasons, the baby should be placed in the cocoon so that the top edge comes around the baby's body, under the armpits.

Abbreviations

See page 126.

Skill level

★ ☆ ☆

To make cocoon

Using US 10½ (6.5mm) needles, cast on 54 sts.

Beg with a k row, work 4 rows in st st.

Row 5: K2, [p2, k2] to end.

Row 6: P2, [k2, p2] to end.

Rep rows 5–6 twice more.

Beg with a k row, work 58 rows in st st.

Row 69: K3, [sl2, k1, p2sso, k6] 5 times, sl2, k1, p2sso, k3. *(42 sts)*

Row 70: Purl.

Row 71: K2, [sl2, k1, p2sso, k4] 5 times, sl2, k1, p2sso, k2. *(30 sts)*

Row 72: Purl.

Row 73: K1, [sl2, k1, p2sso, k2] 5 times, sl2, k1, p2sso, k1. *(18 sts)*

Row 74: [P2tog] to end. *(9 sts)*

Beg with a k row, work 15 rows in st st.

Next row: [P2tog] to end. *(3 sts)*

Break yarn, thread through rem sts, pull firmly, and secure.

To make up

Sew back seam using mattress stitch (see page 124).

Tie knot at the bottom.

Weave in all loose ends.

To make hat

Using US 10½ (6.5mm) needles, cast on 42 sts.
Beg with a k row, work 18 rows in st st.
Row 19: K2, [sl2, k1, p2sso, k4] 5 times, sl2, k1, p2sso, k2. *(30 sts)*
Row 20: Purl.
Row 21: K1, [sl2, k1, p2sso, k2] 5 times, sl2, k1, p2sso, k1. *(18 sts)*
Row 22: Purl.
Row 23: [sl2, k1, p2sso] 6 times. *(6 sts)*
Break yarn, thread through rem sts, pull firmly, and secure.

Ear
(Make 2)
Using US 10 (6mm) needles, cast on 6 sts.
Beg with a k row, work 2 rows in st st.
Row 5: Ssk, k2, k2tog. *(4 sts)*
Row 6: [P2tog] twice. *(2 sts)*
Row 7: [Inc] twice. *(4 sts)*

Row 8: [Inc pwise, p1] twice. *(6 sts)*
Beg with a k row, work 3 rows in st st.
Bind (cast) off pwise.

To make up

Sew back seam of hat using mattress stitch (see page 124).

Fold ear pieces so that the right sides are on the inside. Oversew (see page 125) around curved edges, leaving lower edges open. Turn ears the right way out. Stitch lower edges together and oversew in place.

Weave in all loose ends.

piglet
hot water bottle cozy

Pigs are a firm farmyard favorite and I thought the perfect creature for the hot water bottle treatment. I've chosen a lovely piggy-pink yarn, but the pig color range is huge, so you could just as easily knit yours in pale gray, white… or any other shade you like. This piglet cozy also has the advantage of being the easiest of all the hot water bottle cozies to knit and make up. So if you can already knit a simple hat, this project will be well within your grasp.

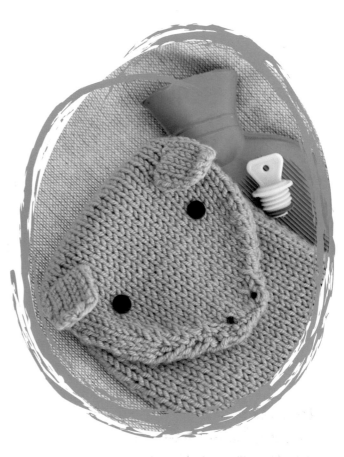

Yarn and materials

Debbie Bliss Rialto Chunky (100% extra-fine merino) bulky (chunky) yarn
  2 x 1¾oz (50g) balls (66yd/60m) in shade 031 Blush

2 x ½in (11mm) dark gray buttons

Oddment of black light worsted (DK) yarn

Black and pink sewing thread

1 x ½in (11mm) snap fastener

Needles and equipment

US 9 (5.5mm) knitting needles

US 6 (4mm) knitting needles

Yarn sewing needle

Large-eyed embroidery needle

Standard sewing needle

Gauge (tension)

14 sts and 22 rows in stockinette (stocking) stitch to a 4-in (10-cm) square on US 9 (5.5mm) needles.

Measurements

The finished cozy is 10in (25cm) long when on the hot water bottle and will fit a standard hot water bottle measuring 9½in (24cm) long (including neck) and 6in (15cm) wide.

Abbreviations

See page 126.

Skill level

★★☆

Rep rows 3–4 once more. *(24 sts)*
Beg with a k row, work 14 rows in st st.
Row 21: K2, k2tog, k to last 4 sts, ssk, k2. *(22 sts)*
Row 22: Purl.
Row 23: K2, k2tog, k to last 4 sts, ssk, k2. *(20 sts)*
Row 24: P2tog, p to last 2 sts, p2tog. *(18 sts)*
Rep rows 23–24 twice more. *(10 sts)*
Row 29: K2, k2tog, k to last 4 sts, ssk, k2. *(8 sts)*
Row 30: Purl.
Bind (cast) off.

Ear

(Make 2)
Using US 6 (4mm) needles, cast on 7 sts.
Beg with a k row, work 6 rows in st st.
Row 7: K2tog, k3, ssk. *(5 sts)*
Row 8: Purl.
Row 9: K2tog, k1, ssk. *(3 sts)*
Row 10: Sl1 pwise, p2tog, psso. *(1 st)*
Break yarn and fasten off.

To make up

Sew the front and back together at the sides and base using mattress stitch (see page 124).

Sew around the head pieces in the same way. Sew the top of the head to the top edge of the back of the body.

Oversew (see page 125) the ears in place using the photograph as a guide.

For the eyes, sew the buttons in place using black thread.

Using black yarn, work two French knots (see page 124) for the nostrils.

Using pink thread, sew one part of the snap fastener in position on the underside of the snout and the other part in a corresponding position on the front of the cozy.

Weave in all loose ends.

To make cozy

Back

Using US 9 (5.5mm) needles, cast on 24 sts.
Beg with a k row, work 42 rows in st st.
Row 43: K2, k2tog, k to last 4 sts, ssk, k2. *(22 sts)*
Beg with a p row, work 3 rows in st st.*
Rep rows 43–46 (last 4 rows) once more. *(20 sts)*
Bind (cast) off.

Front

Work as for back to *.
Row 47: K2, k2tog, k to last 4 sts, ssk, k2. *(20 sts)*
Row 48: Purl.
Knit 3 rows.
Bind (cast) off.

Head

(Make 2)
Using US 9 (5.5mm) needles, cast on 20 sts.
Beg with a k row, work 2 rows in st st.
Row 3: K2, m1, k to last 2 sts, m1, k2. *(22 sts)*
Row 4: Purl.

pumpkin
pickle jar cozy

If you're fed up with boring containers for your tasty Halloween treats, why not jazz up your jars with a few of these creepy cozies? To make your cozy fit narrower or wider jars, simply cast on fewer or more stitches, remembering to take away or add in multiples of four to make sure you can keep to the twist pattern. And if you want a cozy to fit a shorter or taller jar, simply stop knitting sooner or carry on for a bit longer before working the jar edging.

Yarn and materials

Debbie Bliss Rialto DK (100% wool) light wõrsted (DK) yarn

   1 x 1¾oz (50g) ball (115yd/105m) in shade 056 Tangerine (A)

Small amount of black mohair-based yarn for the spiders (B)

Very small amount of 100% polyester toy filling

Needles and equipment

Size US 5 (3.75mm) needles

Size US 3 (3.25mm) needles

Yarn sewing needle

Measurements

The cozy is designed to fit a jar that is 5in (13cm) tall with a circumference of 11½in (29cm). The smaller spiders measure just under ½in (12mm) and the larger one just over ½in (16mm).

Gauge (tension)

24 sts and 28 rows in stockinette (stocking) stitch to a 4-in (10-cm) square on US 5 (3.75mm) needles, using A.

Abbreviations

See page 126.

Skill level

To make cozy

Main piece

Using US 5 (3.75mm) needles, cast on 53 sts in A.

Row 1: [K1, p1, inc, p1] to last st, k1.

Row 2: [P1, k1, p2tog, k1] to last st, p1.

Rep rows 1–2, 16 times more.

Knit 2 rows.

Bind (cast) off.

Small spider

Using US 3 (3.25mm) needles and B doubled, cast on 3 sts.

Row 1: [Inc] to end. *(6 sts)*

Row 2: [Inc] to end. *(12 sts)*

Row 3: [K2tog] to end. *(6 sts)*

Row 4: [K2tog] to end. *(3 sts)*

Bind (cast) off.

Big spider

Using US 3 (3.25mm) needles and B doubled, cast on 4 sts.

Row 1: [Inc] to end. *(8 sts)*

Row 2: [Inc] to end. *(16 sts)*

Knit 2 rows.

Row 5: [K2tog] to end. *(8 sts)*

Row 6: [K2tog] to end. *(4 sts)*

Bind (cast) off.

To make up

To make up main cozy, sew back seam using flat stitch (see page 125).

To make up spiders, put a pinch of polyester toy filling on the shape, run the yarn round the outside, pull firmly, and secure. You can either sew some large stitches on the cozy for the spiders' legs as I have done for the two smaller spiders, or you can secure some short lengths of yarn on the underside of the spider's body, as I have done for the larger spider.

Weave in all loose ends.

flowerpot
cozy and snails

While there's nothing exactly wrong with a plain old flowerpot, there are times when you just want something a little more stylish and fun. And that's exactly where this knitting pattern for a textured pot cozy comes to the rescue. As the yarn is 100 per cent wool, it would be best to make the cozy—and the accompanying friendly and slime-free snails—for indoor plants that only go outside on sunny days.

Yarn and materials

Katia Merino DK (100% merino wool)
light worsted (DK) yarn
  1 x 1¾oz (50g) ball (111yd/102m) in
  shade 055 (A)

Oddment of terracotta light worsted
(DK) yarn (B)

Oddments of light worsted (DK) yarns in
two colors (C) and (D) for each snail

A handful of 100% polyester toy filling

Needles and equipment

US 3 (3.25mm) knitting needles

Yarn sewing needle

US C-2 (2.75mm) crochet hook—or one
of similar size

Gauge (tension)

28 sts and 32 rows in stockinette
(stocking) stitch to a 4-in (10-cm) square
on US 3 (3.25mm) needles.

Measurements

The pot cozy is designed to fit a flowerpot
that is approximately 4¼in (11cm) tall and
has a diameter of 5½in (14cm) but the cozy
is quite stretchy and you can always knit it a
little taller or shorter to fit your particular pot.
The completed snails are 3in (8cm) long.

Abbreviations

See page 126.

Skill level

★★☆

To make cozy

Main piece

Using A, cast on 75 sts.
Row 1: K3, [sl1 pwise, k3] to end.
Row 2: K3, [yf, sl1 pwise, yb, k3] to end.
Row 3: K1, [sl1 pwise, k3] to last 2 sts, sl1 pwise, k1.
Row 4: P1, sl1 pwise, [p3, sl1 pwise] to last st, p1.
Rep rows 1–4, 13 times more.
Break A and join in B.
Row 57: Knit.
Bind (cast) off.

To make snail

The body is knitted from the tail end to the head end.

Body

Cast on 4 sts in C.
Row 1: Inc, k to last 2 sts, inc, k1. *(6 sts)*
Row 2: Purl.
Rep last 2 rows twice more. *(10 sts)*
Beg with a k row, work 16 rows in st st.
Row 23: K2, m1, k6, m1, k2. *(12 sts)*
Beg with a k row, work 15 rows in st st.
Row 29: [Ssk] 3 times, [k2tog] 3 times. *(6 sts)*
Break yarn, thread through rem sts, pull firmly, and secure.

Stalk eyes

Using C and the crochet hook, work two tight 1¼-in
(3-cm) chains (see page 121). Pull the first and last
loops very tightly.

Shell

Cast on 20 sts in D.
Row 1 (WS): Knit.
Beg with a k row, work 4 rows in st st.
Row 6: K2, ssk, k to last 4 sts, k2tog, k2. *(18 sts)*
Row 7: P2tog, p to last 2 sts, p2tog. *(16 sts)*
Row 8: K2, ssk, k to last 4 sts, k2tog, k2. *(14 sts)*
Beg with a p row, work 21 rows in st st.
Row 30: K2, k2tog, k to last 4 sts, ssk, k2. *(12 sts)*
Row 31: Bind (cast) off kwise.

To make up

Join the back seam of the main cozy using flat stitch
(see page 125).

For the snail body, join the seam that will run along the
underneath of the body using mattress stitch (see page
124), stuffing as you go. Thread the stalk eyes through
the top of the head and trim.

Sew the side seam of the shell piece using flat stitch
(see page 125) and stuff lightly. Coil tightly and stitch
the coils in place. Stuff lightly and stitch the front and
back of the shell in place on the body.

Weave in all loose ends.

You can sew snails to the cozy, or push a garden stick
into them through the knitting and push the other end
of the stick into the earth, as in the photograph.

Penguin
hot water bottle cozy

When the nights draw in and the mercury plummets, let this fuzzy baby penguin banish the chill and keep you warm. The yarn I've chosen is as light as a feather, unbelievably soft, and comes in a range of colors that are just right for penguin-creating. There's a bit of sewing together involved but all the pieces are very straightforward to knit, which makes this an ideal project for an advanced beginner or intermediate knitter.

Yarn and materials

Drops Air (70% alpaca, 23% nylon, 7% wool) worsted (Aran) yarn
  1 x 1¾oz (50g) ball (142yd/130m) in each of shade 04 Medium Grey (A), 06 Black (B), and 01 Off-White (C)

Small amount of ocher (ochre) chunky yarn (D) for the beak

A handful of 100% polyester toy filling

3 x ¾in (18mm) gray buttons

Black sewing thread

Needles and equipment

US 7 (4.5mm) knitting needles

Yarn sewing needle

Large-eyed embroidery needle

Standard sewing needle

Gauge (tension)

16 sts and 24 rows in stockinette (stocking) stitch to a 4-in (10-cm) square on US 7 (4.5mm) needles.

Measurements

The finished cozy is 13in (33cm) long when on the hot water bottle and will fit a standard hot water bottle measuring 12¾in (32.5cm) long (including neck) and 8in (20cm) wide.

Abbreviations

See page 126.

Skill level

★★☆

Beg with a k row, work 16 rows in st st.
Row 23: Bind (cast) off 7 sts, k to end. *(29 sts)*
Row 24: Bind (cast) off 7 sts pwise, p to end. *(22 sts)*
Break A and join in B.
Beg with a k row, work 14 rows in st st.
Bind (cast) off.

Wing

(Make 2)
Cast on 10 sts in A.
Beg with a k row, work 14 rows in st st, working a k st at the beg and end of every WS row.
Row 15: K1, ssk, k to last 3 sts, k2tog, k1. *(8 sts)*
Row 16 and every WS row unless stated: K1, p to last st, k1.
Rep rows 15–16 once more. *(6 sts)*
Row 19: K1, ssk, k2tog, k1. *(4 sts)*
Row 21: Ssk, k2tog. *(2 sts)*
Row 22: P2tog. *(1 st)*
Break yarn and fasten off.

Head front

Wind off 1yd (1m) of B.
Cast on 22 sts in B from main ball.
Beg with a k row, work 6 rows in st st.
Row 7: K5 in B, k3 in C, k6 in B using separate length of yarn, k3 in C using yarn from ball center, k5 in B using yarn from ball center.
Row 8: P4 in B, p5 in C, p4 in B, p5 in C, p4 in B.
Row 9: K3 in B, k7 in C, k2 in B, k7 in C, k3 in B.
Row 10: P3 in B, p16 in C, p3 in B.
Row 11: K3 in B, k16 in C, k3 in B.
Row 12: P3 in B, p16 in C, p3 in B.
Rep rows 11–12 once more.
Row 15: K2, ssk in B, k14 in C, k2tog, k2 in B. *(20 sts)*
Row 16: P3 in B, p14 in C, p3 in B.
Row 17: K3 in B, k14 in C, k3 in B.
Row 18: P3 in B, p14 in C, p3 in B.
Row 19: K2, ssk in B, k12 in C, k2tog, k2 in B. *(18 sts)*
Row 20: P3 in B, p12 in C, p3 in B.
Row 21: K2, ssk in B, k10 in C, k2tog, k2 in B. *(16 sts)*
Row 22: P2tog, p1 in B, p10 in C, p2tog, p1 in B. *(14 sts)*
Row 23: K1, ssk in B, ssk, k4, k2tog in C, k2tog, k1 in B. *(10 sts)*
Row 24: P2tog in B, p6 in C, p2tog in B. *(8 sts)*
Bind (cast) off in C.

To make cozy

Front

Cast on 36 sts in A.
Beg with a k row, work 60 rows in st st.
Row 61: Bind (cast) off 7 sts, k to end. *(29 sts)*
Row 62: Bind (cast) off 7 sts pwise, p to end. *(22 sts)*
Beg with a k row, work 14 rows in st st.
Bind (cast) off.

Lower back

Cast on 36 sts in A.
Beg with a k row, work 53 rows in st st.
Row 54: Knit.
Bind (cast) off.

Top back

Cast on 36 sts in A.
Knit 2 rows.
Row 3: K5, bind (cast) off 2 sts, k9 *(10 sts in this group)*, bind (cast) off 2 sts, k9 *(10 sts in this group)*, bind (cast) off 2 sts, k to end. *(30 sts)*
Row 4: K5, turn and cast on 2 sts, turn back, [k10, turn and cast on 2 sts, turn back] twice, turn and cast on 2 sts, k to end. *(36 sts)*
Knit 2 rows.

Head back

Cast on 22 sts in B.

Beg with a k row, work 14 rows in st st.

Row 15: K2, ssk, k to last 4 sts, k2tog, k2. *(20 sts)*

Beg with a p row, work 3 rows in st st.

Row 19: K2, ssk, k to last 4 sts, k2tog, k2. *(18 sts)*

Row 20: Purl.

Row 21: K2, ssk, k to last 4 sts, k2tog, k2. *(16 sts)*

Row 22: P2tog, p to last 2 sts, p2tog. *(14 sts)*

Row 23: K1, [ssk] twice, k4, [k2tog] twice, k1. *(10 sts)*

Row 24: P2tog, p to last 2 sts, p2tog. *(8 sts)*

Bind (cast) off.

Beak

Cast on 10 sts in D.

Knit 2 rows.

Row 3: Ssk, k to last 2 sts, k2tog. *(8 sts)*

Row 4: Purl.

Rep rows 3–4 twice more. *(4 sts)*

Row 9: Ssk, k2tog. *(2 sts)*

Row 10: P2tog. *(1 st)*

Break yarn and fasten off.

To make up

Join side seams and lower edges of the three main cozy pieces with mattress stitch (see page 124), making sure the top back overlaps the lower back.

Oversew (see page 125) the wings in place using the photograph as a guide.

Embroider the eyes in chain stitch (see page 123) using B.

Place head front and back pieces right sides together and oversew sides. Turn the head the right way out, stuff very lightly, and join the top edges using mattress stitch. Oversew top of head to top edge of main cozy. Catch front head behind beak to main part of cozy.

Sew buttons in place.

Weave in all loose ends.

Who wants to sit on a boring old stool when you could be sitting on a tortoise stool? Well certainly not me. This chunky stool cozy is knitted in a thick yarn so comes together really quickly—and the textured back is nothing more than a simple combination of knit and purl stitches, so you don't need to get to grips with anything fancy. So exactly what are you waiting for?

tortoise stool cozy

Yarn and materials

Lion Brand Wool-Ease Thick & Quick super bulky (super chunky) yarn

> 1 x 6oz (170g) ball (106yd/97m) in each of shade 13 Grass (A) and shade 123 Oatmeal (B)

Oddment of off-white and black light worsted (DK) yarns

2 x ⅜in (8mm) black buttons

Several handfuls of 100% polyester toy filling

Needles and equipment

US 10½ (7mm) knitting needles

US 10½ (7mm) 32in (80cm) circular knitting needle

Yarn sewing needle

Large-eyed embroidery needle

Gauge (tension)

11 sts and 14 rows in stockinette (stocking) stitch to a 4-in (10-cm) square on US 10½ (7mm) needles.

Measurements

The cozy is designed to fit an 11-in (28-cm) diameter round stool.

Abbreviations

See page 126.

Skill level

★★☆

To make cozy

Shell

Using US 10½ (7mm) needles, cast on 10 sts in A.
Row 1: Inc, k to last 2 sts, inc, k1. *(12 sts)*
Row 2: Purl.
Row 3: Inc pwise, [k1, p2] to last 2 sts, k1, inc pwise. *(14 sts)*
Row 4: [K2, p1] to last 2 sts, k2.
Row 5: Inc, k to last 2 sts, inc, k1. *(16 sts)*
Row 6: Purl.
Row 7: Inc, [p2, k1] to last 3 sts, p2, inc. *(18 sts)*
Row 8: K1, p1, [k2, p1] to last st, k1.
Row 9: Inc, k to last 2 sts, inc, k1. *(20 sts)*
Row 10: Purl.

Row 11: Inc pwise, p1, [k1, p2] to last 3 sts, k1, p1, inc pwise. *(22 sts)*
Row 12: [P1, k2] to last st, p1.
Row 13: Inc, k to last 2 sts, inc, k1. *(24 sts)*
Row 14: Purl.
Row 15: Inc pwise, [k1, p2] to last 2 sts, k1, inc pwise. *(26 sts)*
Row 16: [K2, p1] to last 2 sts, k2.
Row 17: Knit.
Row 18: Purl.
Row 19: [P2, k1] to last 2 sts, p2.
Row 20: [K2, p1] to last 2 sts, k2.
Row 21: Knit.

Row 22: Purl.

Rep rows 19-22, 3 times more

Row 35: P2tog, [k1, p2] to last 3 sts, k1, p2tog. *(24 sts)*

Row 36: K1, [p1, k2] to last 2 sts, p1, k1.

Row 37: K2tog, k to last 2 sts, ssk. *(22 sts)*

Row 38: Purl.

Row 39: P2tog, p1, [k1, p2] to last 4 sts, k1, p1, p2tog. *(20 sts)*

Row 40: [K2, p1] to last 2 sts, k2.

Row 41: K2tog, k to last 2 sts, ssk. *(18 sts)*

Row 42: Purl.

Row 43: K2tog, [p2, k1] to last 4 sts, p2, ssk. *(16 sts)*

Row 44: [P1, k2] to last st, p1.

Row 45: K2tog, k to last 2 sts, ssk. *(14 sts)*

Row 46: Purl.

Row 47: P2tog, [k1, p2] to last 3 sts, k1, p2tog. *(12 sts)*

Row 48: K1, [p1, k2] to last 2 sts, p1, k1.

Row 49: K2tog, k to last 2 sts, ssk. *(10 sts)*

Bind (cast) off pwise.

Edge

Using US 10½ (7mm) circular needle and with RS facing, pick up and knit 80 sts round entire shell top.

Knit 7 rounds.

Work k1, p1 rib for 3 rounds.

Bind (cast) off, keeping to the k1, p1 pattern.

Head

(Make 2)

Using US 10½ (7mm) needles, cast on 7 sts in B.

Beg with a k row, work 4 rows in st st.

Row 5: K1, m1, k5, m1, k1. *(9 sts)*

Beg with a p row, work 5 rows in st st.

Row 11: K1, k2tog, k3, ssk, k1. *(7 sts)*

Row 12: Purl.

Row 13: K1, k2tog, k1, ssk, k1. *(5 sts)*

Row 14: P2tog, p1, p2tog. *(3 sts)*

Bind (cast) off.

Legs

(Make 4)

Using US 10½ (7mm) needles, cast on 6 sts in B.

Beg with a k row, work 6 rows in st st.

Row 7: K1, ssk, k2tog, k1. *(4 sts)*

Break yarn and thread through rem sts.

Tail

Using US 10½ (7mm) needles, cast on 5 sts in B.

Beg with a k row, work 4 rows in st st.

Row 5: Ssk, k1, k2tog. *(3 sts)*

Row 6: P3tog. *(1 st)*

Break yarn and fasten off.

To make up

Place the two head pieces right sides together and oversew (see page 125) round the curved edges, leaving the cast-on edges open for turning and stuffing. Turn the head the right way out and stuff.

Sew on the button eyes and using the off-white yarn, work a few coils of chain stitch (see page 123) round the buttons.

Using black yarn, work two straight stitches (see page 123) for the mouth.

Join the seams of the legs and tail using mattress stitch (see page 124). Stuff the legs but not the tail. Stitch the head, legs, and tail in place.

Weave in all loose ends.

elephant
hot water bottle cozy

Everyone loves elephants and everyone needs a bit of warming up now and again, so I figured it would be a brilliant idea to create an elephant hot water bottle cozy to keep young ones feeling cheerful on chilly winter nights. I've chosen a gorgeous bluish-gray for this version, as I wanted a nod to true elephant colors. The light and dark grays, and even the pink in this particular yarn would also look amazing, so check out the great color range and see what tickles your fancy.

Yarn and materials

Rowan Cocoon (80% merino wool, 20% mohair) bulky (chunky) yarn
  1 x 3¾oz (100g) ball (126yd/115m) in shade 836 Moon (A)

Small amount of off-white bulky (chunky) yarn (B)

2 x ½in (11mm) dark gray buttons

Black sewing thread

1 x ½in (11mm) snap fastener

Needles and equipment

US 9 (5.5mm) knitting needles

US 7 (4.5mm) knitting needles

Yarn sewing needle

Standard sewing needle

Gauge (tension)

13 sts and 19 rows in stockinette (stocking) stitch to a 4-in (10-cm) square on US 9 (5.5mm) needles.

Measurements

The finished cozy is 10in (25cm) long when on the hot water bottle and will fit a standard hot water bottle measuring 9½in (24cm) long (including neck) and 6in (15cm) wide.

Abbreviations

See page 126.

Skill level

★★☆

To make cozy

Back

Using US 9 (5.5mm) needles, cast on 22 sts in A.
Beg with a k row, work 42 rows in st st.
Bind (cast) off.

Front

Using US 9 (5.5mm) needles, cast on 22 sts in A.
Beg with a k row, work 40 rows in st st.
Knit 2 rows.
Bind (cast) off.

Head

(Make 2)
Using US 9 (5.5mm) needles, cast on 22 sts in A.
Beg with a k row, work 20 rows in st st.
Row 21: K2, ssk, k to last 4 sts, k2tog, k2. *(20 sts)*
Row 22: P2tog, p to last 2 sts, p2tog. *(18 sts)*
Row 23: Bind (cast) off 4 sts, k to end. *(14 sts)*
Row 24: Bind (cast) off 4 sts pwise, p to end. *(10 sts)*
Row 25: Ssk, k to last 2 sts, k2tog. *(8 sts)*
Row 26: Purl.
Rep rows 25–26 once more. *(6 sts)*
Beg with a k row, work 10 rows in st st.
Bind (cast) off.

Ear

(Make 2)
Using US 9 (5.5mm) needles, cast on 20 sts in A.
Beg with a p row, work 3 rows in st st.
Row 4: [K2tog] to end. *(10 sts)*
Row 5: P2tog, p to last 2 sts, p2tog. *(8 sts)*
Row 6: [Ssk] twice, [p2tog] twice. *(4 sts)*
Row 7: [K2tog] twice. *(2 sts)*
Row 8: P2tog. *(1 st)*
Break yarn and fasten off.

Tusks

(Make 2)
Using US 7 (4.5mm) needles, cast on 4 sts in B.
Beg with a k row, work 4 rows in st st.
Row 5: Ssk, k2tog. *(2 sts)*
Row 6: P2tog. *(1 st)*
Break yarn and fasten off.

To make up

Sew the front and back together at the sides and base using mattress stitch (see page 124).

Sew around the head pieces in the same way, leaving the short end of the trunk unstitched. Sew the top of the head to the top edge of the back of the body.

Oversew (see page 125) the ears in place using the photograph as a guide.

Sew the eyes and tusks in place.

Sew one part of the snap fastener in position on the underside of the trunk between the tusks and the other part in a corresponding position on the front of the cozy.

Weave in all loose ends.

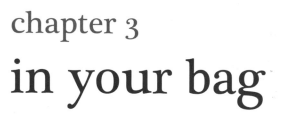

chapter 3

in your bag

teddy bear
bottle cozies

As from right now, drink bottles that are just plain drink bottles are decidedly out of fashion! Armed with just a few balls of light-worsted or DK yarn, you can now create teddy bear cozies for your bottles, so you'll never get your drink muddled up with someone else's again. I've made bears, but with a bit of imagination and some mixing and matching of ideas you'll find in this book, I'm sure you could easily create cats, monkeys, dogs, rabbits…

Yarn and materials

For all three cozies

Sublime Baby Cashmere Merino Silk DK (75% wool, 20% silk, 5% cashmere) light worsted (DK) yarn

    1 x 1¾oz (50g) ball (126yd/115m) in each of shades 124 Splash (A) and 345 Buttermilk (B), and a small amount of bright pink yarn for the cream bear cozy

    1 x 1¾oz (50g) ball (126yd/115m) in each of shades 406 Toot (C) and 275 Nutkin (D), and and a small amount of coral yarn for the brown bear cozy

Debbie Bliss Rialto DK (100% wool) light worsted (DK) yarn

    1 x 1¾oz (50g) ball (115yd/105m) in each of shades 012 Scarlet (E) and 045 (F) Gold, and a small amount of mauve yarn for the yellow bear cozy

Small amount of black light worsted (DK) yarn

1 x ⅜in (11mm) black button for each cozy

Needles and equipment

US 3 (3.25mm) knitting needles

D-3 (3.25mm) crochet hook or one of similar size

Yarn sewing needle

Large-eyed embroidery needle

Gauge (tension)

26 sts and 34 rows in stockinette (stocking) stitch to a 4-in (10-cm) square on US 3 (3.25mm) needles.

Measurements

The finished cozies are 2¾in (7cm) across and are 4½in (11cm) tall and will fit a standard 8½floz (250ml) disposable plastic bottle.

Abbreviations

See page 126.

Skill level

★★✭

To make cream bear cozy

Body and head

Cast on 36 sts in A.

Row 1: [K2, yo twice, p2tog] to end.

Rep row 1, 19 times more.

Break A and join in bright pink yarn.

Knit 2 rows.

Break bright pink yarn and join in B.

Beg with a k row, work 11 rows in st st.

Knit 2 rows.

Bind (cast) off pwise.

Ear

(Make 2)

Cast on 5 sts in B.

Row 1: Knit.

Row 2: Skpo, k1, k2tog. *(3 sts)*

Row 3: Knit.

Row 4: Sk2po. *(1 st)*

Break yarn and fasten off.

Bow

Using the crochet hook, work a 4¾-in (12-cm) crochet chain (see page 121) using bright pink yarn.

To make brown bear cozy

Work as for cream bear cozy using C instead of A, D instead of B, and small amount of coral yarn.

To make yellow bear cozy

Work as for cream bear cozy using E instead of A, F instead of B, and small amount of mauve yarn.

To make up

Sew the back seam of the cozies using flat stitch (see page 125).

Oversew (see page 125) the ears in place using yarn tails.

Work a small coil of about 4 chain stitches (see page 123) for the eyes using black yarn. Use a separated strand of black yarn to sew on the button nose and work a vertical straight stitch (see page 123) beneath it.

Thread the yarn tails of the crochet chain back up the chain to the center and use these to secure the chain into a bow shape and to stitch it in position.

Weave in all loose ends.

With a few balls of fine cotton yarn, you can knit yourself up a huge swarm of cute little lip salve—or lipstick—bug cozies in a trice. Knit them plain or knit them stripy, the choice is yours. True, the needles and yarn used here are on the skinny side, but there's not a lot of knitting involved so the bugs are still really quick to make. And if you fancy it, why not add a thin cord to either side of the body of the cozy so you can sport it round your neck. Don't forget to thread the cord through the head as well to keep it firmly in place.

bug lip-salve cases

Yarn and materials

For all cozies shown and lots more combinations!

Schachenmayr Catania Fine (100% cotton) fingering (4-ply) yarn

  1 x 1¾oz (50g) ball (180yd/165m) in each of shades 00270 Limone (A), 00100 Schwarz (B), 00365 Orange (C), 00280 Loewenzahn (D), and 01002 Tomate (E)

2 x ⅜in (9mm) dark gray buttons for each bug

Needles and equipment

US 1 (2.25mm) knitting needles

Yarn sewing needle

Large-eyed standard sewing needle

B-1 (2.25mm) crochet hook or one of similar size

Gauge (tension)

35 sts and 40 rows in stockinette (stocking) stitch to a 4-in (10-cm) square on US 1 (2.25mm) needles.

Measurements

The cozies are designed to fit a lip salve container measuring approx. 2½–2¾in (just under 7cm) long.

Abbreviations

See page 126.

Skill level

★☆☆

To make lime and black bug cozy

Body

Cast on 18 sts in A.

Beg with a k row, work 6 rows in st st.

Leave A at side of work and join in B.

Knit 2 rows.

Leave B at side of work and use A.

Beg with a k row, work 4 rows in st st.

Rep last 6 rows three times more.

Cont for another 2 rows in st st using A.

Bind (cast) off.

Head

Cast on 22 sts in A.

Beg with a k row, work 8 rows in st st.

Row 9: [K2tog] to end. *(11 sts)*

Row 10: P1, [p2tog] to end. *(6 sts)*

Break yarn, thread through rem sts, pull firmly, and secure.

To make orange and yellow bug cozy

Body
Cast on 18 sts in C.
Beg with a k row, work 32 rows in st st.
Bind (cast) off.

Head
Cast on 22 sts in B.
Break B and join in D.
Beg with a k row, work 8 rows in st st.
Row 9: [K2tog] to end. *(11 sts)*
Row 10: P1, [p2tog] to end. *(6 sts)*
Break yarn, thread through rem sts, pull firmly,
and secure.

To make red, lime, and black bug cozy

Body
Cast on 18 sts in B.
Beg with a k row, work 7 rows in st st.
Row 8: Knit.
Break B and join in E.
Beg with a k row, work 2 rows in st st.
Leave E at side and join in A.
Beg with a k row, work 2 rows in st st.
Keeping to striped pattern, work another 18 rows in
st st, so ending with 2 rows in E.
Bind (cast) off.

Head
Cast on 22 sts in E.
Beg with a k row, work 8 rows in st st.
Row 9: [K2tog] to end. *(11 sts)*
Row 10: P1, [p2tog] to end. *(6 sts)*
Break yarn, thread through rem sts, pull firmly,
and secure.

To make up

Thread yarn tail through cast-on edge of body piece,
pull up tightly, and secure. Sew back seam using flat
stitch (see page 125). Sew back seam of top using
flat stitch.

Sew on button eyes using either A or D.

Using crochet hook and B, make a 1½-in (4-cm) crochet
chain (see page 121) for the antennae. Thread the
chain in and out of the head part of the bug to form the
antennae and trim yarn close to chain.

Weave in all loose ends.

If all clubs looked as cute as these ones, I think there'd be many more people willing to give golf a go. These cozies are knitted in a fabulous shaggy yarn that's really fun to work with—and unlike some shaggy yarns, it doesn't get knotted as soon as you set eyes on it. I've knitted a brown terrier-type dog and a gray poodle one, but with a bit of imagination, I'm sure you could come up with a few other breeds as well—or perhaps some dashing looking mongrels.

doggie golf club cozies

Yarn and materials

Bergère de France Plume (47% polyamide, 42% acrylic, 11% wool) bulky (chunky) yarn
1 x 1¾oz (50g) ball (65yd/60m) in each of shades 34099 Orge (A) and 29316 Graphite (B) for terrier

1 x 1¾oz (50g) ball (65yd/60m) in shade 34094 Gris Clair (C) for poodle

Oddment of black light worsted (DK) yarn (D)

Oddments of light worsted (DK) yarns for collars (E)

Bergère de France Merinos Alpaga (60% merino, 40% alpaca) bulky (chunky) yarn
1 x 1¾oz (50g) ball (71yd/65m) in shade 29899 Ecru (F) for linings

2 x ⅝in (15mm) black buttons for eyes for terrier

2 x ½in (13mm) dark gray buttons for eyes for poodle

Black sewing thread

A small handful of 100% polyester toy filling

Needles and equipment

US 10 (6mm) knitting needles

Yarn sewing needle

Large eyed embroidery needle

Standard sewing needle

2 x stitch markers or small safety pins

Gauge (tension)

14 sts and 18 rows in stockinette (stocking) stitch to a 4-in (10-cm) square on US 10 (6mm) needles using A or B.

Measurements

The cozies will fit most standard golf clubs.

Abbreviations

See page 126.

Skill level

★★★

Terrier

Head

Cast on 24 sts in A.
Row 1: K10, inc, k2, inc, k to end. *(26 sts)*
Row 2: Purl.
Row 3: K11, m1, k4, m1, k to end. *(28 sts)*
Beg with a p row, work 11 rows in st st, putting st marker or small safety pin at either end of 9th of these rows.

Row 15: K2, ssk, k to last 4 sts, k2tog, k2. *(26 sts)*
Row 16: Purl.
Row 17: K2, ssk, k6, ssk, k2, k2tog, k6, k2tog, k2. *(22 sts)*
Row 18: Purl.
Row 19: K2, ssk, k to last 4 sts, k2tog, k2. *(20 sts)*
Row 20: Purl.
Rep rows 19–20 once more. *(18 sts)*
Row 23: K2, [ssk] 3 times, k2, [k2tog] 3 times, k2. *(12 sts)*

Row 24: Purl.

Break A and join in D, using yarn doubled.

Row 25: K2, [ssk] twice, [k2tog] twice, k2. *(8 sts)*

Row 26: [Ssk] twice, [k2tog] twice. *(4 sts)*

Break yarn, thread through rem sts, and pull up securely.

Muzzle

Cast on 14 sts in A.

Knit 4 rows.

Bind (cast) off loosely.

Ear

(Make 2)

Cast on 5 sts in B.

Knit 14 rows.

Row 15: Ssk, k1, k2tog. *(3 sts)*

Row 16: Sk2po. *(1 st)*

Break yarn and fasten off.

Neck

Cast on 24 sts in A.

Work 18 rows in k1, p1 rib.

Break A and join in E, using yarn doubled.

Knit 4 rows.

Bind (cast) off.

Lining

Cast on 22 sts in F.

Beg with a k row, work 12 rows in st st and put row marker at either end of last row.

Row 13: K2, ssk, k to last 4 sts, k2tog, k2. *(20 sts)*

Row 14: Purl.

Rep rows 13–14, 3 times more. *(14 sts)*

Row 21: K2, [ssk] twice, k2, [k2tog] twice, k2. *(10 sts)*

Row 22: Purl.

Row 23: K1, [ssk] twice, [k2tog] twice, k1. *(6 sts)*

Row 24: [P2tog] three times. *(3 sts)*

Break yarn, thread through rem sts, and secure.

Poodle

Work main head and neck as for terrier, using C instead of A and D. Make lining as for terrier.

Ear

(Make 2)

Cast on 5 sts in C.

Knit 8 rows.

Row 9: K1, m1, k3, m1, k1. *(7 sts)*

Knit 11 rows.

Row 21: K1, ssk, k1, k2tog, k1. *(5 sts)*

Row 22: Ssk, k1, k2tog. *(3 sts)*

Row 23: S1, k2tog, psso. *(1 st)*

Break yarn and fasten off.

Topknot

Cast on 14 sts in C.

Knit 8 rows.

Row 9: [K2tog] to end. *(7 sts)*

Break yarn, thread through rem sts, and pull up securely.

To make up

Fold main head piece in half and oversew (see page 125) from nose end to stitch markers or small safety pins.

Fold neck piece in half and sew neck seam using flat stitch (see page 125). Stitch top edge of collar around head opening, so seam is at the back of the head.

Oversew the ears in place.

Oversew the button eyes in place using standard black sewing thread.

For the terrier, join the short edges of muzzle piece and oversew one long edge in place around the nose, keeping the short seam on the underside of the nose. Oversew the second long edge in place slightly back from the nose, stuffing lightly as you go.

For the poodle, gather the topknot piece along the cast-on edge, stuff lightly, and join the row edge sides together using mattress stitch (see page 124). Oversew in place on the top of the head.

Weave in all loose ends.

big cat
phone cozies

Knitted phone cozies are perfect if you want to bring a dash of homespun charm to your high-tech phone. These cozies have a simple flap that tucks in the back so, when you need to, you can get out your phone in a hurry. And when it's snuggled inside, your phone will stay safe and secure. If the fancy takes you, why not work out how many other animals you can create using this basic pattern and some carefully chosen alternative yarns and facial features?

Yarn

Lion Brand Wool-Ease (80% acrylic, 20% wool) worsted (Aran) yarn

1 x 3oz (85g) ball (196yd/180m) in each of shades 159 Mustard (A) and 199 Pumpkin (B) for the lion

1 x 3oz (85g) ball (196yd/180m) in each of shades 171 Gold (A) and 153 Black (B) for the tiger

Small amount of light worsted (DK) yarn in off-white for both cozies

Small amount of worsted (Aran) or light worsted (DK) yarn in black for the lion

Needles and equipment

US 6 (4mm) knitting needles

US 3 (3.25mm) knitting needles (tiger cozy only)

US 2/3 (3mm) knitting needles (lion cozy only)

Yarn sewing needle

Large-eyed embroidery needle

Gauge (tension)

19 sts and 25 rows in stockinette (stocking) stitch to a 4-in (10-cm) square on US 6 (4mm) needles.

Measurements

The cozies are designed to be a fairly snug fit on a phone that measures just under 5½in by just over 2½in (14 x 7cm). The finished cozy measures 6 x 3¼in (15 x 8cm) unstretched. For phones of other sizes, you will need to adjust the pattern.

Abbreviations

See page 126.

Skill level

★★★

To make cozy

Lion

Back

Using US 6 (4mm) needles, cast on 18 sts in A.
Row 1: [K1, p1] to end.
Rep row 1, 3 times more.
Beg with a k row, work 32 rows in st st.
Bind (cast) off.

Front

Using US 6 (4mm) needles, cast on 18 sts in A.
Row 1: Knit.
Row 2: K2, p to last 2 sts, k2.

Rep rows 1–2, 4 times more.
Beg with a k row, work 36 rows in st st.
Bind (cast) off.

Mane

Using US 2/3 (3mm) needles, cast on 38 sts in B.
Bind (cast) off 2 sts, *sl rem st from right-hand to left-hand needle and cast on another 2 sts.
Bind (cast) off 4 sts.*
Rep from * to * to last st.
K1, bind (cast) off 1 st so there is 1 st on needle.
Fasten off.

To make up

Sew the side and bottom seams using mattress stitch (see page 124), remembering that the first 10 rows of the front, where you have worked the garter stitch border, form a flap to tuck in at the back.

Sew the mane in place using slip stitch.

Using black yarn, make two French knots (see page 124) for the eye centers. Using the off-white yarn, work a circle of chain stitch (see page 123) round each French knot.

Use black yarn to work a small square for the nose in chain stitch and add some straight stitches (see page 123) for the mouth, using the photograph as a guide.

Weave in all loose yarn ends.

Tiger

When knitting the stripes, you don't have to break the yarn at the end of each stripe. You can take it up the side of your work, catching it from time to time at the side at the start of your rows.

Back

Using US 6 (4mm) needles, cast on 18 sts in A.
Row 1: [K1, p1] to end.
Rep row 1, 3 times more.
Rows 5–8: Beg with a k row, work 4 rows in st st.
Leave A at side and join in B.
Rows 9–10: Beg with a k row, work 2 rows in st st.
Leave B at side and pick up A.
Rows 11–14: Beg with a k row, work 4 rows in st st.
Leave A at side and pick up B.
Rows 15–16: Beg with a k row, work 2 rows in st st.
Rep rows 11–16 (last 6 rows) twice more.
Break B, cont in A.
Beg with a k row, work 8 rows in st st.
Bind (cast) off.

Front

Using US 6 (4mm) needles, cast on 18 sts in A.
Row 1: Knit.
Row 2: K2, p to last 2 sts, k2.
Rep rows 1–2, 4 times more.
Rows 15–24: Beg with a k row, work 14 rows in st st.
Leave A at side and join in B.
Rows 25–26: Beg with a k row, work 2 rows in st st.

Leave B at side and pick up A.
Rows 27–30: Beg with a k row, work 4 rows in st st.
Leave A at side and pick up B.
Rows 31–32: Beg with a k row, work 2 rows in st st.
Rep rows 27–32 (last 6 rows) once more.
Break B, cont in A.
Beg with a k row, work 8 rows in st st.
Bind (cast) off.

Ear

(Make 2)
Using US 3 (3.25mm) needles, cast on 5 sts in A.
Knit 3 rows.
Row 4: Ssk, k1, k2tog. *(3 sts)*
Row 5: K3tog. *(1 st)*
Fasten off.

To make up

Sew the side and bottom seams using mattress stitch (see page 124), remembering that the first 10 rows of the front, where you have worked the garter stitch border, form a flap to tuck in at the back.

Oversew the ears in place.

Using B, make two French knots (see page 124) for the eye centers. Using the off-white yarn, work a circle of chain stitch (see page 123) round each French knot.

Use B to work the nose in straight stitches (see page 123) using the photograph as a guide.

Weave in all loose ends.

When you're fed up with all the novelty key cases that you can find in the stores, it's time to start knitting your own. This fishy key cozy—which can be attached to a keyring or worn on a cord around your neck—is the perfect safe haven for any slim key measuring up to 2¾in (7cm).

shark key cozy

Yarn

Debbie Bliss Baby Cashmerino (55% wool, 33% acrylic, 12% cashmere) light worsted (DK) yarn
  1 x 1¾oz (50g) ball (137yd/125m) in shade 202 Light Blue

Small amounts of light worsted (DK) yarns in each of black and light gray

Needles and equipment

US 2/3 (3mm) knitting needles

Yarn sewing needle

Large-eyed embroidery needle

Stitch markers

Gauge (tension)

27 sts and 36 rows in stockinette (stocking) stitch to a 4-in (10-cm) square on US 2/3 (3mm) needles.

Measurements

The shark cozy is 4in (10cm) long and can be used to conceal a standard door or similar type of key up to 2¾in (7cm) long. Please note that it is not designed for typical car keys as they are too wide.

Abbreviations

See page 126.

Skill level

★★★

To make cozy

Body

Cast on 8 sts.

Row 1: [Inc] to end. *(16 sts)*

Beg with a p row, work 3 rows in st st.

Row 5: [K2, m1] 3 times, k1, m1, k2, m1, k1, [m1, k2] 3 times. *(24 sts)*

Beg with a p row, work 9 rows in st st, marking the 6th, 12th, 13th, and 19th sts of the 6th of these 9 rows (which is row 11 overall) with stitch markers or contrasting thread on the RS of work.

Row 15: K1, k2tog, k6, ssk, k2, k2tog, k6, ssk, k1. *(20 sts)*

Beg with a p row, work 5 rows in st st.

Row 21: K1, k2tog, k4, ssk, k2, k2tog, k4, ssk, k1. *(16 sts)*

Beg with a p row, work 5 rows in st st.

Row 27: K1, k2tog, k2, ssk, k2, k2tog, k2, ssk, k1. *(12 sts)*

Row 28: Purl.

Row 31: K9, turn.

Row 32: P6, turn and work on these 6 sts only, leaving rem sts on needle.

*Beg with a k row, work 4 rows in st st.

Next row: Ssk, k2, k2tog. *(4 sts)*

Next row: [P2tog] twice. *(2 sts)*

Next row: Ssk. *(1 st)*

Fasten off.*

Carefully rearrange sts on needle so that the needles face in opposite directions and point to outer edges of work. Then with WS facing, bring needles around and put sts from RH needle onto LH needle.

Rejoin yarn to RS of work and rep from * to *.

Dorsal fin

With RS facing, run a knitting needle down through your work between the two central marked sts on row 11 and out again further on toward the tail, so that you have 8 running threads on your needle. You will use these running threads as sts.

Row 1: Knit.

Row 2: Ssk, k to last 2 sts, k2tog. *(6 sts)*

Rep row 2 once more. *(4 sts)*

Row 4: Ssk, k2tog. *(2 sts)*

Row 5: K2tog. *(1 st)*

Fasten off.

Pectoral fin

In the same way that you picked up running stitches for the dorsal fin, run your needle into your work at one of the remaining markers and out again further on toward the tail, so that you have 4 running threads on your needle.

Knit 4 rows.

Row 5: Ssk, k2tog. *(2 sts)*

Row 6: K2tog. *(1 st)*

Fasten off.

Work the second fin in the same way.

To make up

Sew the main body seam using mattress stitch (see page 124), taking care to leave a small hole at the head end of the shark.

Sew ¼–½in (0.5–1cm) along the lower outside edge of each tail fin to give them a bit of shape, making sure the central opening remains large enough to stretch out to release your key.

Using black yarn, work French knots (see page 124) for the eye centers and work a ring of chain stitch (see page 123) around these centers using the main yarn.

Using a single separated strand of light gray yarn, work three small vertical straight stitches (see page 123) on each side of the shark between the eye and the pectoral fin for the gills.

Using black yarn, work two straight stitches for the mouth, using the photograph as a guide.

flamingo bottle cozy

Who wouldn't want this elegant flamingo livening up a drinks cabinet and adding a dash of 1950s' cocktail vibes to the whole proceedings? The cozy will help your bottle stand out from the crowd and keep your red wine at just the right temperature. And the lacy stitch is pretty easy to do, once you've had a bit of practice. Who knows? If you get hooked, you could find yourself knitting a whole colony of these avian beauties.

Yarn and materials

Patons Merino Extrafine DK (100% wool) light worsted (DK) yarn
 1 x 50g (1¾oz) ball (131yd/120m) in shade 134 Coral (A)

Small amount of light worsted (DK) yarn in each of white (B) and black (C)

Small amount of 100% polyester toy filling

Needles and equipment

US 5 (3.75mm) knitting needles

Yarn sewing needle

Large-eyed embroidery needle

Gauge (tension)

26 sts and 32 rows in stockinette (stocking) stitch to a 4-in (10-cm) square on US 5 (3.75mm) needles.

Measurements

The cozy will fit a standard 75cl glass bottle such as a wine bottle. The finished cozy is 11½in (29cm) long.

Abbreviations

See page 126.

Skill level

★★★

To make cozy

Body

Cast on 52 sts in A.

Row 1: K1, [k2tog, yo, k1, yo, skpo] to last st, k1.

Row 2: Purl.

Rep rows 1–2, 29 times more.

Row 61: Knit.

Row 62: Purl.

Row 63: [K2tog] to end. *(26 sts)*

Beg with a p row, work 5 rows in st st.

Row 69: K2, [k2tog, k3] 4 times, k2tog, k2. *(21 sts)*

Beg with a p row, work 24 rows in st st.

Row 94: Knit.

Bind (cast) off.

Wing

(Make 2)

Cast on 12 sts in A.

Row 1: K1, [k2tog, yo, k1, yo, skpo] to last st, k1.

Row 2: Purl.

Rep rows 1–2, 7 times more.

Row 17: [K2tog] 3 times, [skpo] 3 times. *(6 sts)*

Row 18: Purl.

Row 19: K2tog, k2, skpo. *(4 sts)*

Row 20: [P2tog] twice. *(2 sts)*

Row 21: K2tog.

Break yarn and fasten off.

Beak

Cast on 12 sts in B.

Beg with a k row, work 2 rows in st st.

Break B and join in C.

Row 3: K1, k2tog, k to last 3 sts, skpo, k1. *(10 sts)*

Row 4: Purl.

Rep rows 3–4 twice more. *(6 sts)*

Row 9: K1, k2tog, skpo, k1. *(4 sts)*

Row 10: [P2tog] twice. *(2 sts)*

Row 11: K2tog. *(1 st)*

Fasten off.

To make up

Sew the main back body seam using flat stitch (see page 125).

Oversew (see page 125) the wings in place on either side of the body along the cast-on edge—you will find this easier to do if you have the cozy on the bottle.

Sew the seam of the beak and stuff lightly. Oversew the beak in place so the seam is on the underside.

Using C, work two French knots (see page 124) for the centers of eyes. Split a 12-in (30-cm) length of B into two thinner strands and use these to work a circle of chain stitch (see page 123) around the eye centers.

Weave in all loose ends.

octopus apple cozy

If you want to add a bit of creativity and fun to a healthy packed lunch or the family fruit bowl, you've landed on just the right page. This friendly-looking octopus is knitted in a silky yarn that's firm enough to create a safe environment for your fruit—and it comes in a range of beautiful colors to make some very handsome octopuses. I've chosen a slightly unconventional pink just to add a bit of vibrancy, but you may prefer one of the subtle shades of blue or green. As always, it's just a matter of choice.

Yarn and materials

Lion Brand Martha Stewart Extra Soft Wool Blend (65% acrylic, 35% wool) worsted (Aran) yarn
 1 x 3½oz (100g) ball (164yd/150m) in shade 502 Flamingo

Small amount of light worsted (DK) yarn in black

1 x ¾in (18mm) round pink button (to match yarn)

Needles and equipment

US 6 (4mm) knitting needles

US 8 (5mm) knitting needles

D-3 (3.25mm) crochet hook or one of a similar size

Stitch markers (optional)

Yarn sewing needle

Large-eyed embroidery needle

Gauge (tension)

19 sts and 25 rows in stockinette (stocking) stitch to a 4-in (10-cm) square on US 6 (4mm) needles.

Measurements

The cozy is designed to fit an average size apple. It measures 3½in (9cm) from the top to the bottom and each leg is approx. 3½in (9cm) when stretched out.

Abbreviations

See page 126.

Skill level

★★★

To make cozy

Body

Using US 6 (4mm) needles, cast on 9 sts.
Row 1: [Inc] to end. *(18 sts)*
Row 2: Purl.
Rep rows 1–2 once more. *(36 sts)*
Beg with a k row, work 4 rows in st st.
Row 9: K4, [m1, k7] 4 times, m1, k4. *(41 sts)*
Beg with a p row, work 3 rows in st st.
Mark beg and end of last row with a stitch marker or contrasting thread.

Beg with a k row, work a further 6 rows in st st.
Row 19: K3, [sl2, k1, p2sso, k5] 4 times, sl2, k1, p2sso, k3. *(31 sts)*
Row 20: Purl.
Row 21: K2, [sl2, k1, p2sso, k3] 4 times, sl2, k1, p2sso, k2. *(21 sts)*
Row 22: Purl.
Row 23: K1, [sl2, k1, p2sso, k1] 4 times, sl2, k1, p2sso, k1. *(11 sts)*
Row 24: Purl.
Bind (cast) off.

Legs

Using yarn doubled and US 8 (5mm) needles, cast on 16 sts.

Bind (cast) off 15 sts.

*Slip single rem st from RH to LH needle.

Cast on 15 sts.

Bind (cast) off 15 sts.*

Rep from * to * 6 times more to make eight legs.

Fasten off.

To make up

Sew the back seam of the cozy from the cast-on edge up to the stitch markers.

Then with the right side of the work facing you, pick up and knit 12 sts from the top corner down to the base of the opening. Then pick up and knit another 12 sts from this point to the second top corner. Bind (cast) off, leaving a reasonably long yarn tail (this will be used to form the button loop).

Using black yarn, work two French knots (see page 124) for the eye centers. Separate an 18-in (45-cm) length of the main yarn into two thinner strands and use these to embroider a coil of chain stitch (see page 123) around each eye center. (I have worked the eyes slightly off center as I liked the look of them on the ends of the ridges formed by the double decreases, but you can sew yours more centrally if you prefer.)

To make the button loop, use the crochet hook to make a ¾-in (2-cm) chain (see page 121) from a yarn tail and fasten the loose end to the main cozy. Stitch the button in place.

Form the leg piece into a circle and slip stitch in place at the base of the body.

Weave in all loose ends.

whale phone cozy

Fuzzy and small rather than smooth and gigantic, this is a blue whale with a difference, and the ideal cozy disguise for your phone. I love the subtle blue yarn and the whale's friendly face. And I think this cozy would make a fabulous gift for any animal-loving smart-phone addict.

Yarn and materials

Lion Brand Wool-Ease (80% acrylic, 20% wool) worsted (Aran) yarn

    1 x 3oz (85g) ball (196yd/180m) in shade 123 Seaspray

Small amount of light worsted (DK) yarn in dark gray

1 x ⅜in (8mm) black dome button

A tiny amount of 100% polyester toy filling

Needles and equipment

US 3 (3.25mm) knitting needles

Yarn sewing needle

Large-eyed embroidery needle

Gauge (tension)

24 sts and 32 rows in stockinette (stocking) stitch to a 4-in (10-cm) square on US 3 (3.25mm) needles.

Measurements

The cozy is designed to be a fairly snug fit on a phone that measures just under 5½in by just over 2½in (14 x 6.5cm). The finished cozy measures 8 x 3¼in (20.5 x 8cm) unstretched and including tail. For phones of other sizes, you will need to adjust the pattern.

Abbreviations

See page 126.

Skill level

★★☆

To make cozy

Front

Cast on 22 sts.

Beg with a k row, work 45 rows in st st.

Row 46: Bind (cast) off 14 sts pwise, p to end. *(8 sts)*

Beg with a k row, work 4 rows in st st.

Row 51: K7, WT.

Row 52 and every WS row: Purl.

Row 53: K6, WT.

Row 55: K5, WT.

Row 57: K4, WT.

Row 59: K3, WT.

Row 61: K2, WT.

Row 63: K1, WT.

Row 64: Purl.

Beg with a k row, work 4 rows in st st.

Shape tail fin

Row 69: K1, ssk, k2, k2tog, k1. *(6 sts)*

Row 70: Purl.

Row 71: K1, m1, k to last st, m1, k1. *(8 sts)*

Row 72: Purl.

Rep rows 71–72 twice more. *(12 sts)*

Row 77: K1, m1, k5, turn and cont on these 7 sts only, leaving rem sts on needle.

*Beg with a p row, work 3 rows in st st.

Next row: Ssk, k3, k2tog. *(5 sts)*

Next row: P2tog, p1, p2tog. *(3 sts)*

Next row: Sl1, k2tog, psso. *(1 st)**

Fasten off.

Rejoin yarn to rem sts on RS of work.

Next row: K5, m1, k1. *(7 sts)*

Work from * to * once more.

Tail end of back

Cast on 22 sts.

Row 1: [K1, p1] to end.

Rep row 1, 3 times more.

Beg with a k row, work 30 rows in st st.

Row 35: Bind (cast) off 14 sts, k to end. *(8 sts)*

Beg with a p row, work 4 rows in st st.

Row 40: P7, WT.

Row 41 and every RS row: Knit.

Row 42: P6, WT.

Row 44: P5, WT.

Row 46: P4, WT.

Row 48: P3, WT.

Row 50: P2, WT.

Row 52: P1, WT.

Row 53: Knit.

Beg with a p row, work 3 rows in st st.

Shape tail fin as for front.

Head end of back

Cast on 22 sts.

Row 1: [K1, p1] to end.

Rep row 1, 3 times more.

Beg with a k row, work 10 rows in st st.

Bind (cast) off.

To make up

With the front and tail end of the back pieces right sides together, oversew (see page 125) around tail. Turn the piece the right way out and join remaining seams using mattress stitch (see page 124).

Place the head end of the back piece in position, making sure it overlaps the other back piece, and continue joining the cozy together using mattress stitch.

Stuff the tail lightly.

Sew the eye in position.

Using the gray yarn, embroider the mouth in chain stitch (see page 123) on the front of the cozy, using the photograph as a guide.

Weave in all loose ends.

frog tissue case

Disguise and beautify that everyday essential tissue packet with a bespoke frog cozy, complete with luscious mouth and goggle eyes. These cozies are quick to make, a bit of fun, and would make an ideal small gift or Christmas stocking filler. I love this beautiful soft green yarn from Rowan, but the frog would be equally unforgettable in "tropical frog" shades such as yellow, turquoise, or even a variegated rainbow yarn. So have a rifle through your yarn stash and create your own new species.

Yarn and materials

Rowan Pure Wool Superwash DK (100% wool) light worsted (DK) yarn
1 x 1¾oz (50g) ball (137yd/125m) in shade 0104 Marl (A)

Small amount of light worsted (DK) yarn in each of pink, off-white, and black

Small amount of 100% polyester toy filling

Needles and equipment

US 8 (5mm) knitting needles

US 3 (3.25mm) knitting needles

Yarn sewing needle

Large-eyed embroidery needle

Gauge (tension)

15 sts and 24 rows in stockinette (stocking) stitch to a 4-in (10-cm) square on US 8 (5mm) needles, using yarn doubled.

Measurements

The finished cozy measures 4¾ x 2¾in (12 x 7cm) and is designed to fit a standard small packet of tissues.

Abbreviations

See page 126.

Skill level

★☆☆

To make cozy

Main part
Using yarn doubled and US 8 (5mm) needles, cast on 20 sts in pink yarn.
Break yarn and join in A, using it doubled.
Beg with a k row, work 32 rows in st st.
Break A and rejoin pink yarn, using it doubled.
Bind (cast) off.

Eye hood
(Make 2)
Using US 3 (3.25mm) needles and single strand of A, cast on 3 sts.
Row 1: [Inc] 3 times. *(6 sts)*
Row 2: Purl.
Row 3: K1, [m1, k1] to end. *(11 sts)*
Row 4: Knit.
Bind (cast) off.

Eyeball

(Make 2)

Using US 3 (3.25mm) needles and off-white light worsted (DK) yarn, cast on 4 sts.

Row 1: [Inc] 4 times. *(8 sts)*

Row 2: Purl.

Row 3: K1, [inc] 6 times, k1. *(14 sts)*

Row 4: Purl.

Row 5: [K2tog] to end. *(7 sts)*

Row 6: Purl.

Row 7: K2tog, sl2, k1, p2sso, k2tog. *(3 sts)*

Break yarn, thread it through rem sts, and pull up securely.

To make up

With the right side of your work facing outward, fold the two short edges of the main piece together to form the mouth and oversew (see page 125) the edges of the mouth together 1¼in (3cm) at each side.

Turn the piece so that the right sides are on the inside and the mouth is just to one side of the horizontal center line. Oversew the two short sides then turn the piece the right way out.

Sew the eye hoods in place so that the bound- (cast-) off edges form the outer rim of the eye hood. Join the side seam of the eyeballs using flat stitch (see page 125), stuffing lightly as you go. Place the eyeballs in the eye hoods. Stitch in place along the part of the eyeball that meets the top of the main cozy and along the outer rim of the eye hood. Using the black yarn, work a small circle of chain stitch (see page 123) for the eye centers.

Weave in all loose ends.

snake recorder cozy

Keep your recorder clean and safe from bumps and scratches in its very own snakey cozy. I've knitted this one in bright red and yellow to resemble a coral snake, but you could knit yours in your favorite color combination to make it really distinctive. Or simply stick to plain green if you're a more subdued type of musician.

Yarn and materials

Wendy Mode Chunky (50% wool, 50% acrylic) bulky (chunky) yarn
  1 x 3½oz (100g) ball (153yd/140m)
  in each of shades 220 Coal (A),
  257 Lemon Squash (B), and
  262 Hot Chilli (C)

Small amount of 100% polyester toy filling

Needles and equipment

US 8 (5mm) knitting needles

Yarn sewing needle

Large-eyed embroidery needle

F-5 (3.75mm) crochet hook or one of a similar size

Gauge (tension)

14 sts and 19 rows in stockinette (stocking) stitch to a 4-in (10-cm) square on US 8 (5mm) needles.

Measurements

The cozy is designed to fit a standard recorder approx. 12¾in (32.5cm) long. The finished cozy is 15in (38cm) long excluding the tongue.

Abbreviations

See page 126.

Skill level

★☆☆

To make cozy

Body
Cast on 7 sts in A.
Row 1: [Inc] to end. *(14 sts)*
Beg with a p row, work 11 rows in st st.
*Leave A at side and join in B.
Beg with a k row, work 2 rows in st st.
Leave B at side and join in C.
Beg with a k row, work 6 rows in st st.
Leave C at side and join in B.
Beg with a k row, work 2 rows in st st.
Leave B at side and join in A.
Beg with a k row, work 6 rows in st st.*
Rep from * to * twice more.
Row 61: [K1, p1] to end.
Rep row 61, 3 times more.
Bind (cast) off keeping to the k1, p1 pattern.

Head outer piece
Cast on 14 sts in A.
Row 1: [K1, p1] to end.
Rep row 1 once more.
Row 3: K2, [m1, k2] to end. *(20 sts)*
Beg with a p row, work 9 rows in st st.
*Row 13: K2, [k2tog] 4 times, [ssk] 4 times, k2. *(12 sts)*
Row 14: Purl.
Row 15: [K2tog] 3 times, [ssk] 3 times. *(6 sts)*
Break yarn, thread it through rem sts, and pull up securely.

Head inner piece
Cast on 20 sts in A.
Beg with a k row, work 6 rows in st st.
Work as for head outer piece from * to end.

Tongue
Using 3 strands separated from a 12-in (30-cm) length of C, make a 3½-in (9-cm) crochet chain (see page 121).

> When knitting the stripes, you don't have to break the yarn at the end of each stripe. You can take it up the side of your work, catching it from time to time at the side at the start of your rows.

To make up

Sew the body seam using mattress stitch (see page 124) and A.

Sew the seams of the two head pieces using mattress stitch. Place a very small handful of toy filling in the outer head and spread it up the sides slightly, almost as if you were lining the piece with it. Place the inner head piece inside the outer head piece so they are wrong sides together. Slip stitch the two pieces together from the inside, around the top of the ribbing of the outer head piece.

Separate a 12-in (30-cm) length of A into two lengths, one with 3 strands and one with 2 strands: the latter can be thrown away. Using the former, work two French knots (see page 124) for the eye centers. Using a similarly separated length of B, work a coil of chain stitch (see page 123) round each eye center, using the photograph as a guide.

Fold the crochet chain for the tongue in half and join the first ⅜in (1cm) of the folded end together. Sew the tongue in place.

If you like, join the head to the body with a loose stitch or two to make sure the head doesn't go missing.

Weave in all loose ends.

chapter 4

on your desk

raccoon
tablet cozy

Just because they're high tech, I don't think that tablets should be left out in the cold when it comes to hand-knitted cozies. But I've made sure this one looks so super smart in black, gray, and white, so he'll look at home in a busy office as well as somewhere a bit more homely. I've used a hardwearing and washable thick yarn—so you can rustle up this raccoon cover pretty quickly and easily clean him down if you need to.

Yarn and materials

James C Brett Chunky with Merino (70% acrylic, 20% polyamide, 10% merino) bulky (chunky) yarn

    1 x 3½oz (100g) ball (164yd/150m) in each of shades 09 (A) and 03 (B)

Sirdar Country Style DK (40% nylon, 30% wool, 30% acrylic) light worsted (DK) yarn

    1 x 1¾oz (50g) ball (170yd/155m) in shade 417 Black (C)

1 x ¾in (22mm) black button

1 x ½in (11mm) snap fastener

Needles and equipment

US 9 (5.5mm) knitting needles

Yarn sewing needle

Large-eyed embroidery needle

Gauge (tension)

15 sts and 21 rows in stockinette (stocking) stitch to a 4-in (10-cm) square on US 9 (5.5mm) needles, using A or B.

Measurements

The cozy is designed to fit a tablet measuring approx. 9½ x 7¼in (24 x 18.5cm). For tablets of other sizes you will need to adjust the pattern.

Abbreviations

See page 126.

Skill level

★★✫

To make cozy

Front
Cast on 28 sts in A.
Beg with a k row, work 46 rows in st st.
Knit 4 rows.
Bind (cast) off.

Back
Cast on 28 sts in A.
Beg with a k row, work 48 rows in st st.
Bind (cast) off.

Face

Cast on 28 sts in A.

Beg with a k row, work 4 rows in st st.

Break A and join in B.

Row 5: K2, k2tog, k to last 4 sts, ssk, k2. *(26 sts)*

Row 6: Purl.

Rep rows 5–6 once more. *(24 sts)*

Break B and join in C, using yarn doubled.

Row 9: K2, k2tog, k to last 4 sts, ssk, k2. *(22 sts)*

Row 10: Purl.

Rep rows 9–10 twice more. *(18 sts)*

Break C and join in B.

*Row 15: K2, k2tog, k to last 4 sts, ssk, k2. *(16 sts)*

Row 16: Purl.

Rep rows 15–16, 4 times more. *(8 sts)*

Row 25: K2, k2tog, ssk, k2. *(6 sts)*

Row 26: P2tog, p2, p2tog. *(4 sts)*

Row 27: Ssk, k2tog. *(2 sts)*

Break yarn, thread it through rem sts, and secure.

Head underside

Cast on 28 sts in A.

Beg with a k row, work 4 rows in st st.

Row 5: K2, k2tog, k to last 4 sts, ssk, k2. *(26 sts)*

Row 6: Purl.

Rep rows 5–6, four times more. *(18 sts)*

Break A and join in B.

Cont as for face from * to end.

Ear

(Make 2)

Cast on 6 sts in A.

Beg with a k row, work 4 rows in st st.

Row 5: Ssk, k2, k2tog. *(4 sts)*

Row 6: [P2tog] twice. *(2 sts)*

Row 7: K2tog. *(1 st)*

Row 8: Inc pwise. *(2 sts)*

Row 9: [Inc] twice. *(4 sts)*

Row 10: Purl.

Row 11: K1, m1, k2, m1, k1. *(6 sts)*

Beg with a p row, work 4 rows in st st.

Bind (cast) off kwise.

To make up

Embroider the eyes in chain stitch (see page 123) using B.

Place face and head underside pieces right sides together and oversew (see page 125) sides. Turn the head the right way out and join the top edges using mattress stitch (see page 124).

Fold the ear pieces so the right sides are together and oversew along sides leaving the lower edges open for turning. Turn the right way out, oversew along lower edge, and stitch the ears in position.

Join side seams of main cozy in flat stitch (see page 125) and lower edges in mattress stitch.

Oversew top of head to top edge of back of main cozy. Sew button in place for the nose. Sew the top of the snap fastener under the button and the corresponding part on the front of the cozy.

Weave in all loose ends.

panda mug hug

With their monochrome coats and friendly faces, it's no wonder that these bamboo-munching giants are some of the most adorable creatures on the planet. And now you can create your own cuddly mug-hugging versions for both a standard-size cup and something a bit more giant, just like the creature itself. Not only do these mug hugs look great, they'll help keep your favorite drinks warm, too.

Yarn and materials

Wendy Mode Chunky (50% wool, 50% acrylic) bulky (chunky) yarn
1 x 3½oz (100g) ball (153yd/140m) in each of shades 202 Vanilla (A) and 220 Coal (B)

Small amounts of contrasting chunky yarns for the collars and bows

1 x ¾in (18mm) gray button for each cozy

Needles and equipment

US 8 (5mm) knitting needles

Yarn sewing needle

Large-eyed embroidery needle

Stitch markers

Gauge (tension)

16 sts and 22 rows in stockinette (stocking) stitch to a 4-in (10-cm) square on US 8 (5mm) needles.

Measurements

The smaller cozy fits a standard ½ pint (300ml) and the larger cozy fits a 1 pint (600ml) mug. The smaller cozy is 3¼in (8.5cm) deep and has a 9½in (24cm) circumference. The larger cozy is 4¼in (10.5cm) deep and has an 11½in (29cm) circumference.

Abbreviations

See page 126.

Skill level

★★☆

Figures for the larger cozy are given in brackets after the figures for the smaller cozy

To make mug hug

Main part

Cast on 38(46) sts using yarn for collar.
Knit 2 rows.
Break collar yarn and join in A.

Beg with a p row, work 16(20) rows in st st, noting instructions below.
For smaller size, mark beg and end of 5th and 12th rows on RH side with stitch markers or contrasting thread.
For larger size, mark beg and end of 6th and 15th rows on RH side with stitch markers or contrasting thread.
Bind (cast) off kwise.

Tab

For the smaller cozy, with RS facing pick up and knit 6 sts evenly between 5th and 12th rows, checking that the tab knitted here will fit neatly through your mug handle and adjusting the position if necessary.
Row 2: K2, p2, k2.
Row 3: Knit.
Row 4: K2, p2, k2.
Rep rows 3–4 twice more.
Row 9: K2, bind (cast) off 2 sts, k to end. *(4 sts)*
Row 10: K2, turn and cast on 2 sts, turn back and k to end. *(6 sts)*
Row 11: Knit.
Row 12: Bind (cast) off tightly.

For the larger cozy, with RS facing pick up and knit 8 sts evenly between 6th and 15th row, checking that the tab knitted from here will fit centrally through the mug handle and adjusting the position if necessary.

Row 2: K2, p4, k2.

Row 3: Knit.

Row 4: K2, p4, k2.

Rep rows 3–4 twice more.

Row 9: K3, bind (cast) off 2 sts, k to end. *(6 sts)*

Row 10: K3, turn and cast on 2 sts, turn back and k to end. *(8 sts)*

Row 11: Knit.

Row 12: Bind (cast) off tightly.

Ear

(Make 2)

Cast on 6 sts in B.

Beg with a k row, work 4 rows in st st.

Row 5: K2tog, k2, ssk. *(4 sts)*

Row 6: [P2tog] twice. *(2 sts)*

Row 7: [Inc] twice. *(4 sts)*

Row 8: [Inc pwise, p1] twice. *(6 sts)*

Beg with a k row, work 4 rows in st st.

Bind (cast) off.

Eye patch

(Make 2)

Cast on 2 sts in B.

Row 1: [Inc] twice. *(4 sts)*

Beg with a p row, work 3 rows in st st.

Row 5: K2tog, ssk. *(2 sts)*

Row 6: P2tog. *(1 st)*

Fasten off.

Bow

Cast on 22 sts in yarn used for collar.

Bind (cast) off.

To make up

Fold the ear pieces in half, right sides together and oversew (see page 125) round the curved edges, leaving the flat edge open for turning. Turn the ears the right way out and slip stitch together at the base. Oversew in position.

Oversew the eye patches in position using the photograph as a guide.

Separate a 12-in (30-cm) length of B into two thinner strands. Use these to work a French knot (see page 124) for the eye centers in the middle of each eye patch—making sure you can see its position on the black eye patch. Using a similarly separated length of A, work a circle of chain stitch (see page 123) around the eye centers.

Using a separated length of B, work a coil of chain stitches for the nose and add a straight stitch (see page 123) at the bottom, using the photograph as a guide.

Join the top and bottom edges of the side seams using flat stitch (see page 125).

Join the two short ends of the bow piece together and secure in place on the front of the collar by working a few straight stitches over the center point.

Sew the button in position.

Weave in all loose ends.

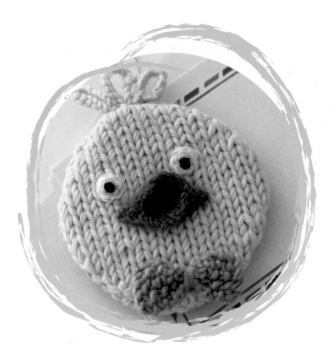

If you're fed up with your earphones getting tangled and tattered, it's time to make them a cheerful duck cozy. The cozy is knitted using standard light worsted (DK) yarn, but because it is used double, the cozy is thick enough to keep its precious contents really safe. And if you feel inspired, with a little imagination, you could whip up a whole cast of earphone cozy characters; the possibilities are endless.

duck earphones cozy

Yarn

Patons Merino Extrafine DK (100% wool) light worsted (DK) yarn
  1 x 1¾oz (50g) ball (131yd/120m) in shade 120 Sundance

Small amount of light worsted (DK) yarn in a color of your choice for the bow

Small amount of light worsted (DK) yarn in each of deep orange, off-white, and black

Needles and equipment

US 6 (4mm) knitting needles

US 2/3 (3mm) knitting needles

D-3 (3.25mm) crochet hook or one of a similar size

Yarn sewing needle

Large-eyed embroidery needle

Gauge (tension)

18 sts and 26 rows on stockinette (stocking) stitch to a 4-in (10-cm) square on US 6 (4mm) needles, using yarn doubled.

Measurements

The cozy is 3½in (9cm) in diameter.

Abbreviations

See page 126.

Skill level

★☆☆

To make cozy

Front

Using US 6 (4mm) needles and yarn doubled, cast on 7 sts.
Row 1: Inc, k to last 2 sts, inc, k1. *(9 sts)*
Row 2: Purl.
Rep rows 1–2 once more. *(11 sts)*
Row 5: K1, m1, k to last st, m1, k1. *(13 sts)*
Row 6: Purl.
Rep rows 5–6 twice more. *(17 sts)*
Beg with a k row, work 4 rows in st st.
*Row 15: K2tog, k to last 2 sts, ssk. *(15 sts)*
Row 16: Purl.
Rep rows 15–16, 3 times more. *(9 sts)*
Row 23: K2tog, k to last 2 sts, ssk. *(7 sts)*
Bind (cast) off pwise.

Back

(Make 2)

Using US 6 (4mm) needles and yarn doubled, cast on
17 sts.

Row 1: K1, [p1, k1] to end.
Row 2: P1, [k1, p1] to end.

Beg with a k row, work 2 rows in st st.

Work as for front from * to end.

Beak

Using US 2/3 (3mm) needles and deep orange yarn,
cast on 6 sts.

Row 1: Inc, k to last 2 sts, inc, k1. *(8 sts)*
Row 2: Purl.
Row 3: K1, m1, k to last st, m1, k1. *(10 sts)*

Beg with a p row, work 3 rows in st st.

Row 7: K1, k2tog, k4, ssk, k1. *(8 sts)*
Row 8: P2tog, p4, p2tog. *(6 sts)*

Bind (cast) off.

Head tuft

Using crochet hook and single strand of yarn, make a
6½in (17-cm) crochet chain (see page 121).

Bow

Using US 2/3 (3mm) needles and chosen yarn, cast on
5 sts.

Row 1: K1, [p1, k1] to end.

Rep row 1, 13 times more.

Bind (cast) off pwise.

To make up

Place back pieces on front pieces so that the right
sides are together and the two back pieces overlap.
Oversew (see page 125) around the entire edge. Turn
the cozy the right way out and position the right
way up, so that the top piece of the back of the head
overlaps the bottom piece.

Arrange crochet chain into three loops and sew in
position on top of head.

Using black yarn, work French knots (see page 124) for
the eye centers. Using off-white yarn, work a circle of
chain stitch (see page 123) around each French knot.

Fold the beak in half so the cast-on and bound- (cast-)
off edges meet and the right side of the piece is on the
outside. Join side edges for ¼in (0.5cm) to shape beak.
Sew the beak to the cozy along this fold line, with the
cast-on edge at the top of the beak.

Join the bow to the cozy by working a few straight
stitches (see page 123) over the center.

Weave in all loose ends.

These adorable kitty-faced cup hugs will keep little hands cool and the drink inside warm—which has got to be a great combination. They're knitted in seed (moss) stitch, which makes a lovely firm knit but is still super-easy to work. I've added some readymade bows to mine—but you could also opt for fish-shaped buttons or even a tiny bell.

kitten cup hugs

Yarn and materials

For all three cozies

Patons Merino Extrafine DK (100% wool) light worsted (DK) yarn
  1 x 1¾oz (50g) ball (131yd/120m) in each of the following shades:
  125 Orange (A), 123 Apricot (B), 190 Light Grey Heather (C), and 102 Cream (D)

Small oddment of dark gray or black light worsted (DK) yarn for features

A selection of small readymade ribbon bows, measuring approx. 1¼ x 1¼in (3 x 3cm) or some narrow ribbon to make your own

Sewing thread for sewing on bows

Needles and equipment

US 3 (3.25mm) knitting needles

Yarn sewing needle

Large-eyed embroidery needle

Standard sewing needle

Gauge (tension)

26 sts and 34 rows in stockinette (stocking) stitch to a 4-in (10-cm) square on US 3 (3.25mm) needles.

Measurements

The finished cozies are 3¾in (9.5cm) across and 1¾in (4.5cm) tall (excluding ears) and will fit a small disposable cup that is 3¾in (9.5cm) tall and has a top circumference of 9¼in (23.5cm).

Abbreviations

See page 126.

Skill level

★☆☆

To make marmalade kitten cup hug

Main part
Cast on 47 sts in A.
Break A and join in B.
Row 1: [K1, p1] to last st, k1.
Rep row 1, 15 times more.
Break B and join in A.
Row 17: [K1, p1] to last st, k1.
Bind (cast) off kwise.

Ears
With RS facing and using yarn A, pick up and knit 6 sts from 15th to 20th stitch along bound- (cast-) off edge.
Row 2: Purl.
Row 3: Ssk, k2, k2tog. *(4 sts)*
Row 4: Purl.
Row 5: Ssk, k2tog. *(2 sts)*
Row 6: P2tog. *(1 st)*
Break yarn and fasten off.

Work the second ear in same way, but from 28th st to 33rd st along bound- (cast-) off edge.

To make gray kitten cup hug

Work main part and ears as for marmalade kitten, using C instead of A and B.

Eye patch

Cast on 5 sts in D.
Row 1: [K1, p1] twice, k1.
Rep row 1, 4 times more.
Bind (cast) off pwise.

To make white kitten cup hug

Work main part and ears as for marmalade kitten using D instead of A and B.

To make up

Sew the eye patch onto the gray cozy, following the photograph.

Work a small coil of about 4 chain stitches (see page 123) for the eyes using dark gray or black yarn.

Using a divided length of the same yarn, work the noses and mouths using straight stitches (see page 123).

Sew the short sides of the cozy together using flat stitch (see page 125).

Sew the bows in place using sewing thread.

Weave in all loose ends.

salamander pencil case

Every so often, you want to create something that sets you apart from the rest of humanity, and this salamander pencil case will help you do just that. He's practical and fun, so makes the ideal desk companion.

Yarn and materials

Rowan Pure Wool Superwash DK (100% wool) light worsted (DK) yarn

1 x 1¾oz (50g) ball (137yd/125m) in shade 019 Avocado (A)

Small amount of light worsted (DK) yarns in each of coral, black, and off-white

6in (15cm) black metal zipper

Small amount of 100% polyester toy filling

Needles and equipment

US 3 (3.25mm) knitting needles

Yarn sewing needle

Large-eyed embroidery needle

Gauge (tension)

22 sts and 34 rows in stockinette (stocking) stitch to a 4-in (10-cm) square on US 3 (3.25mm) needles.

Measurements

The finished pencil case is 9½in (24cm) long.

Abbreviations

See page 126.

Skill level

★★★

To make cozy

Upper body

Cast on 9 sts in A.

Row 1: Inc, k to last 2 sts, inc, k1. *(11 sts)*
Row 2: Purl.
Row 3: K1, m1, k to last 2 sts, m1, k1. *(13 sts)*
Row 4: Purl.
Rep rows 3–4, 4 times more. *(21 sts)*
Beg with a k row, work 10 rows in st st.*
Row 23: K1, [p1, k1] to end.
Row 24: P1, [k1, p1] to end.
Row 25: P1, [k1, p1] to end.
Row 26: K1, [p1, k1] to end.
Rep rows 23–26, 6 times more.
**Row 51: P2tog, [k1, p1] to last 3 sts, k1, p2tog. *(19 sts)*
Row 52: K1, [p1, k1] to end.
Rep rows 51–52 twice more. *(15 sts)*
Row 57: K1, [p1, k1] to end.
Row 58: P1, [k1, p1] to end.
Row 59: K2tog, [p1, k1] to last 3 sts, p1, k2tog. *(13 sts)*
Row 60: P1, [k1, p1] to end.
Row 61: P1, [k1, p1] to end.
Row 62: K1, [p1, k1] to end.

Row 63: K1, [p1, k1] to end.
Row 64: P1, [k1, p1] to end.
Row 65: P1, [k1, p1] to end.
Row 66: K1, [p1, k1] to end.
Rep rows 63–66 twice more.
Row 75: P2tog, [k1, p1] to last 3 sts, k1, p2tog. *(11 sts)*
Row 76: K1, [p1, k1] to end.
Row 77: K1, [p1, k1] to end.
Row 78: P1, [k1, p1] to end.
Row 79: K2tog, [p1, k1] to last 3 sts, p1, k2tog. *(9 sts)*
Row 80: P1, [k1, p1] to end.
Row 81: P1, [k1, p1] to end.
Row 82: K1, [p1, k1] to end.
Row 83: P2tog, [k1, p1] to last 3 sts, k1, p2tog. *(7 sts)*
Row 84: K1, [p1, k1] to end.
Row 85: K1, [p1, k1] to end.
Row 86: P1, [k1, p1] to end.
Row 87: K2tog, p1, k1, p1, k2tog. *(5 sts)*
Row 88: [P1, k1] twice, p1.
Row 89: [P1, k1] twice, p1.
Row 90: [K1, p1] twice, k1.
Row 91: P2tog, k1, p2tog. *(3 sts)*
Row 92: P3tog. *(1 st)*
Fasten off.

Lower body

Work as for upper body to *.
Beg with a k row, work a further
28 rows in st st.
Work from ** to end.

Leg

(Make 4)
Cast on 8 sts in A.
Beg with a k row, work 8 rows in
st st.
Row 9: [K2tog] to end. *(4 sts)*
Break yarn, thread it through rem
sts, and pull up securely.

Mouth

Cast on 38 sts in coral yarn.
Row 1: Inc, k to last 2 sts, inc, k1.
(40 sts)
Row 2: Purl.
Row 3: K2, bind (cast) off 30 sts,
k1 (2 sts in last group on needle).
(4 sts)
Row 4: P2, turn work and cast on 36 sts, turn work back
and p2. *(40 sts)*
Row 5: K2tog, k to last 2 sts, ssk. *(38 sts)*
Row 6: Purl.
Bind (cast) off.

To make up

Place the two body pieces right sides together and
oversew (see page 125) close to the edge from the
beginning of the seed (moss) stitch on the upper body
down both sides to the tip of the tail.

Place the zipper under the mouth piece and, using
coral yarn and medium-length running stitches, sew it
in position along both long edges.

Slip stitch the mouth in place on the main cozy.

Sew up the seams for the legs, stuff them lightly, and
oversew in place.

Using the black yarn, work two French knots (see
page 124) for the eye centers. Using off-white yarn,
work two coils of chain stitch (see page 123) round
the eye centers.

Weave in all loose ends.

koala
book cozy

Koalas are one of the world's most adorable creatures, and now you can knit one of your very own to keep your favorite book safe and secure. I've knitted the cozy in a lovely yarn that contains a large amount of super-soft alpaca. And I can guarantee this will be one of the most popular projects in the book. I think you'll find that once you've knitted one of these cozies, all your friends will be asking you to knit them one too. So needles at the ready, one and all.

Yarn and materials

Drops Air (70% alpaca, 23% polyamide, 7% wool) worsted (Aran) yarn

    1 x 1¾oz (50g) ball (142yd/130m) in each of shades 04 Medium Grey (A) and 01 Off-White (B)

Small amount of light worsted (DK) yarn in black (C)

A handful of 100% polyester toy filling

2 x ⅜in (8mm) black dome buttons

1 x ½in (11mm) snap fastener

Needles and equipment

US 6 (4mm) knitting needles

US 2/3 (3mm) knitting needles

Yarn sewing needle

Large-eyed embroidery needle

Gauge (tension)

19 sts and 27 rows in stockinette (stocking) stitch to a 4-in (10-cm) square on US 6 (4mm) needles.

Measurements

The cozy is designed to fit a standard size paperback book, measuring approx. 5 x 7¾in (13 x 19.5cm) and about 1in (2.5cm) thick. The finished cozy measures 6 x 9in (15 x 23cm).

Abbreviations

See page 126.

Skill level

★★☆

To make cozy

Front
Using US 6 (4mm) needles, cast on 30 sts in A.
Beg with a k row, work 22 rows in st st.
Break A and join in B.
Beg with a k row, work 36 rows in st st.
Row 59: [K1, p1] to end.

Rep row 59, 3 times more.
Bind (cast) off.

Back
Using US 6 (4mm) needles, cast on 30 sts in A.
Beg with a k row, work 62 rows in st st.
Bind (cast) off.

Head

(Make 2)

Using US 6 (4mm) needles, cast on 27 sts in A.

Beg with a k row, work 18 rows in st st.

Row 19: K2, k2tog, k to last 4 sts, ssk, k2. *(25 sts)*

Row 20: Purl.

Row 21: K2, k2tog, k to last 4 sts, ssk, k2. *(23 sts)*

Row 22: P2tog, p to last 2 sts, p2tog. *(21 sts)*

Rep last 2 rows twice more. *(13 sts)*

Bind (cast) off.

Arm

(Make 2)

Using US 6 (4mm) needles, cast on 12 sts in A.

Beg with a k row, work 12 rows in st st.

Row 13: [K2tog] to end. *(6 sts)*

Break yarn, thread through rem sts, and pull up securely.

Ear

(Make 2)

Using US 6 (4mm) needles, cast on 14 sts in A.

Beg with a k row, work 6 rows in st st.

Row 7: [K2tog] to end. *(7 sts)*

Break yarn, thread through rem sts, and pull up securely.

Nose

Using US 2/3 (3mm) needles, cast on 5 sts in C.

Row 1: Inc, k to last 2 sts, inc, k1. *(7 sts)*

Row 2: Purl.

Rep rows 1–2 once more. *(9 sts)*

Row 5: Knit.

Row 6: Purl.

Row 7: K1, k2tog, k3, ssk, k1. *(7 sts)*

Row 8: Purl.

Row 9: K1, k2tog, k1, ssk, k1. *(5 sts)*

Row 10: P2tog, p1, p2tog. *(3 sts)*

Row 11: K3tog. *(1 st)*

Fasten off.

To make up

Join the main front and back pieces together at the base and sides using mattress stitch (see page 124).

Join the two head pieces together, oversewing (see page 125) the curves from the inside and using mattress stitch at the sides and base. Oversew the head in position on the top of the body back.

Oversew the nose in place, stuffing it lightly as you go. To make the outside edge of the nose really neat, work a line of chain stitch (see page 123) using C around it.

Join the arm seams using mattress stitch. Sew the arms in place on the side seams and work some straight stitches (see page 123) in C to secure the arms on the tummy and to represent the claws.

Sew the seams on the ears, stuff them lightly, and secure in place using the photograph as a guide.

Sew the button eyes in position.

Sew the snap fastener in position on the underneath part of the head and in a corresponding position on the body front.

Weave in all loose ends.

meerkat
e-reader cozy

The world is full of all kinds of cozies to keep your e-readers safe when you're on the move, but who wants something staid and boring when, with a bit of knitting time and know-how, you can rustle up a meerkat to do the job? This cute little member of the mongoose family is always on the lookout, so it seemed the ideal creature to keep watch over your precious gadget.

Yarn and materials

Hayfield Chunky with Wool (80% acrylic, 20% wool) bulky (chunky) yarn
 1 x 3½oz (100g) ball (158yd/145m) in each of shades 695 Roasted (A) and 772 Stoneacre (B)

Small amount of light worsted (DK) yarn in black

2 x ⅜in (8mm) black dome buttons

1 x ½in (11mm) snap fastener

Needles and equipment

US 8 (5mm) knitting needles

US 5 (3.75mm) knitting needles

Stitch markers (optional)

Yarn sewing needle

Large-eyed embroidery needle

Gauge (tension)

15 sts and 23 rows in stockinette (stocking) stitch to a 4-in (10-cm) square on US 8 (5mm) needles.

Measurements

The cozy is designed to fit an e-reader measuring 4¾ x 6¾ x ⅜in (12 x 17 x 1cm), or a very similar size. The finished cozy measures 4¾ x 6¾in (12 x 17cm).

Abbreviations

See page 126.

Skill level

★★☆

To make cozy

Body front

Using US 8 (5mm) needles, cast on 20 sts in A.
Beg with a k row, work 10 rows in st st.
Break A and join in B.
Beg with a k row, work 25 rows in st st.
Row 36: Knit.
Bind (cast) off.

Body back and head front

Using US 8 (5mm) needles, cast on 20 sts in A.
Beg with a k row, work 36 rows in st st.
Mark beg and end of last row with a stitch marker
or a short length of contrasting yarn or thread.
Beg with a k row, work 2 rows in st st.
Break A.
Row 39: K7 in B; rejoin A and k6; k to end in B using
yarn from center of ball.
Row 40: P8 in B; p4 in A; k to end in B.
Row 41: K1, k2tog, k6 in B; k2 in A; k6, ssk, k1 in B.
(18 sts)
Break A and B from outer ball and cont in B.

Row 42: P2tog, p to last 2 sts, p2tog. (16 sts)
Row 43: K1, k2tog, k to last 3 sts, ssk, k1. (14 sts)
Row 44: P2tog, p to last 2 sts, p2tog. (12 sts)
Row 45: K1, k2tog, k to last 3 sts, ssk, k1. (10 sts)
Row 46: Purl.
Rep rows 45–46 once more. (8 sts)
Break B, rejoin A and work rem of piece in A.
Row 49: K2tog, k4, ssk. (6 sts)
Row 50: Purl.
Row 51: K2tog, k2, ssk. (4 sts)
Row 52: Purl.
Row 53: K2tog, ssk. (2 sts)
Row 54: P2tog. (1 st)
Fasten off.

Head underside

Using US 8 (5mm) needles, cast on 20 sts in A.
Beg with a k row, work 4 rows in st st.
Row 5: K1, k2tog, k to last 3 sts, ssk, k1. (18 sts)
Row 6: P2tog, p to last 2 sts, p2tog. (16 sts)
Row 7: K1, k2tog, k to last 3 sts, ssk, k1. (14 sts)
Row 8: P2tog, p to last 2 sts, p2tog. (12 sts)
Row 9: K1, k2tog, k to last 3 sts, ssk, k1. (10 sts)
Row 10: Purl.
Rep rows 9–10 once more. (8 sts)
Row 13: K2tog, k4, ssk. (6 sts)
Row 14: Purl.
Row 15: K2tog, k2, ssk. (4 sts)
Row 16: Purl.
Row 17: K2tog, ssk. (2 sts)
Row 18: P2tog. (1 st)
Fasten off.

Arm

(Make 2)
Using US 8 (5mm) needles, cast on 7 sts in B.
Beg with a k row, work 10 rows in st st.
Row 11: K2tog, sl2, k1, p2sso, ssk. (3 sts)
Break yarn, thread through rem sts, and pull up securely.

Ear

(Make 2)
Divide a 12-in (30-cm) length of A into two thinner
strands.

Using US 5 (3.75mm) needles and one thin strand, cast on 4 sts.

Knit 4 rows.

Row 5: Ssk, k2tog. *(2 sts)*

Row 6: Ssk. *(1 st)*

Fasten off.

To make up

Join side seams using mattress stitch (see page 124), matching top of body front with stitch markers on body back and head piece.

With right sides together, oversew (see page 125) across the base.

Weave in all central loose yarn ends on the reverse side of the front of head. Place the head underside piece on the head front so that the right sides are together and oversew at the sides leaving the top edges open. Turn right sides out and slip stitch top edge of head underside in place along top of head front.

Using a separated strand of A, work a small flattened circle of chain stitch (see page 123) for the eye patches, using the photograph as a guide. Sew the buttons inside the circle.

Using black yarn, work a coil of chain stitch around the tip of the face for the nose.

Oversew the ears in place on the side of head.

Sew the arm seams and stitch the arms in place on the sides of the body.

Sew the snap fastener in position on the underside of the nose and in a corresponding position on the body front.

Weave in all loose ends.

techniques

On the following pages you'll find the basic knitting techniques that you will need for most of the patterns in this book. The knitting needles, yarn, and other items that you need to make each project are listed at the beginning of the relevant pattern instructions. You can substitute the yarn recommended in a pattern with the same weight of yarn in a different brand, but you will need to check the gauge (tension) (see opposite). When calculating the quantity of yarn you require, it is the length of yarn in each ball that you need to check, rather than the weight of the ball; the length of yarn in each ball of the recommended project yarn is given in the materials list for the pattern.

If you are substituting brands for a very small amount of yarn—for example, to embroider a nose or eyes—this will hardly affect the look of your project at all, and it is very sensible to use up yarns you have in your stash.

Gauge (tension)

A gauge (tension) is given with each pattern to help you make your item the same size as the sample. The gauge (tension) is given as the number of stitches and rows you need to work to produce a 4-in (10-cm) square of knitting.

Using the recommended yarn and needles, cast on 8 stitches more than the gauge (tension) instruction asks for—so if you need to have 10 stitches to 4in (10cm), cast on 18 stitches. Working in pattern as instructed, work eight rows more than is needed. Bind (cast) off loosely.

Lay the swatch flat without stretching it. Lay a ruler across the stitches as shown, with the 2in (5cm) mark centered on the knitting, then put a pin in the knitting at the start of the ruler and at the 4in (10cm) mark: the pins should be well away from the edges of the swatch. Count the number of stitches between the pins. Repeat the process across the rows to count the number of rows to 4in (10cm).

If the number of stitches and rows you've counted is the same as the number asked for in the instructions, you have the correct gauge (tension). If you do not

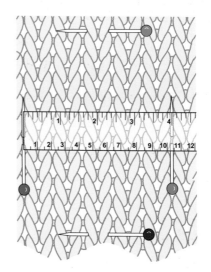

have the same number then you will need to change your gauge (tension).

To change gauge (tension) you need to change the size of your knitting needles. A good rule of thumb to follow is that one difference in needle size will create a difference of one stitch in the gauge (tension). You will need to use larger needles to achieve fewer stitches and smaller ones to achieve more stitches.

Holding needles

If you are a knitting novice, you will need to discover which is the most comfortable way for you to hold your needles.

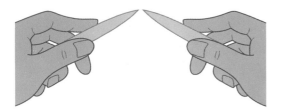

Like a knife

Pick up the needles, one in each hand, as if you were holding a knife and fork—that is to say, with your hands lightly over the top of each needle. As you knit, you will tuck the blunt end of the right-hand needle under your arm, let go with your hand, and use your hand to manipulate the yarn, returning your hand to the needle to move the stitches along.

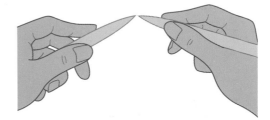

Like a pen

Now try changing the right hand so you are holding the needle as you would hold a pen, with your thumb and forefinger lightly gripping the needle close to its pointed tip and the shaft resting in the crook of your thumb. As you knit, you will not need to let go of the needle but simply slide your right hand forward to manipulate the yarn.

Holding yarn

As you knit, you will be working stitches off the left-hand needle and onto the right-hand needle, and the yarn you are working with needs to be tensioned and manipulated to produce an even fabric. To hold and tension the yarn you can use either your right or left hand, depending on the method you are going to use to make the stitches.

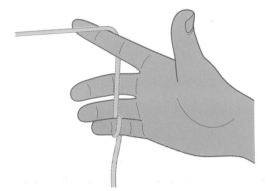

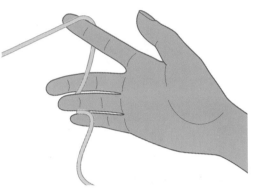

Yarn in right hand

To knit and purl in the US/UK style (see pages 114 and 115), hold the yarn in your right hand. You can wind the yarn around your fingers in different ways, depending on how tightly you need to hold it to achieve an even gauge (tension). Try both ways shown to find out which works best for you.

To hold the yarn tightly (left), wind it right around your little finger, under your ring and middle fingers, then pass it over your index finger, which will manipulate the yarn.

For a looser hold (right), catch the yarn between your little and ring fingers, pass it under your middle finger, then over your index finger.

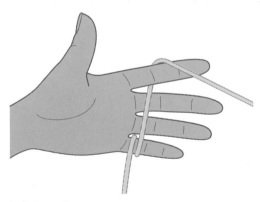

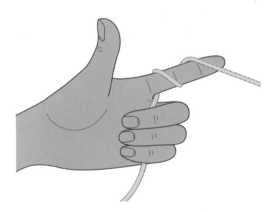

Yarn in left hand

To knit and purl in the continental style (see pages 114 and 115), hold the yarn in your left hand. This method is sometimes easier for left-handed people to use, though many left-handers are quite comfortable knitting with the yarn in their right hand. Try the ways shown to find out which works best for you.

To hold the yarn tightly (left), wind it right around your little finger, under your ring and middle fingers, then pass it over your index finger, which will manipulate the yarn.

For a looser hold (right), fold your little, ring, and middle fingers over the yarn, and wind it twice around your index finger.

Making a slip knot

You will need to make a slip knot to form your first cast-on stitch.

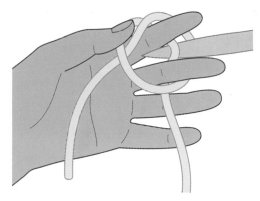 

1 With the ball of yarn on your right, lay the end of the yarn on the palm of your left hand and hold it in place with your left thumb. With your right hand, take the yarn around your top two fingers to form a loop. Take the knitting needle through the back of the loop from right to left and use it to pick up the strand nearest to the yarn ball, as shown in the diagram. Pull the strand through to form a loop at the front.

2 Slip the yarn off your fingers, leaving the loop on the needle. Gently pull on both yarn ends to tighten the knot. Then pull on the yarn leading to the ball of yarn to tighten the knot on the needle.

Casting on (cable method)

There are a few methods of casting on but the one used for the projects in this book is the cable method, which uses two needles.

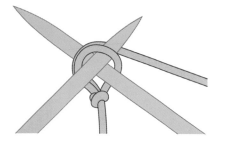  

1 Make a slip knot as shown above. Put the needle with the slip knot into your left hand. Insert the point of the other needle into the front of the slip knot and under the left-hand needle. Wind the yarn from the ball of yarn around the tip of the right-hand needle.

2 Using the tip of the needle, draw the yarn through the slip knot to form a loop. This loop is the new stitch. Slip the loop from the right-hand needle onto the left-hand needle.

3 To make the next stitch, insert the tip of the right-hand needle between the two stitches. Wind the yarn over the right-hand needle, from left to right, then draw the yarn through to form a loop. Transfer this loop to the left-hand needle. Repeat until you have cast on the right number of stitches for the project.

Knit stitch

There are only two stitches to master in knitting; knit stitch and purl stitch. Most people in the English-speaking world knit using a method called English (or American) knitting. However, in parts of Europe, people prefer a method known as Continental knitting.

US/UK style

1 Hold the needle with the cast-on stitches in your left hand, and then insert the point of the right-hand needle into the front of the first stitch from left to right. Wind the yarn around the point of the right-hand needle, from left to right.

2 With the tip of the right-hand needle, pull the yarn through the stitch to form a loop. This loop is the new stitch.

3 Slip the original stitch off the left-hand needle by gently pulling the right-hand needle to the right. Repeat these steps till you have knitted all the stitches on the left-hand needle. To work the next row, transfer the needle with all the stitches into your left hand.

Continental style

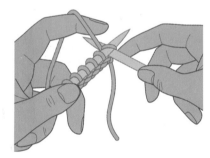 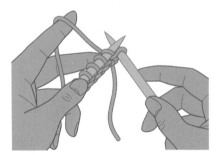 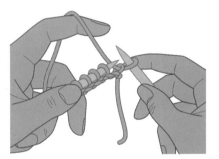

1 Hold the needle with the stitches to be knitted in your left hand, and then insert the tip of the right-hand needle into the front of the first stitch from left to right. Holding the yarn fairly taut with your left hand at the back of your work, use the tip of the right-hand needle to pick up a loop of yarn.

2 With the tip of the right-hand needle, bring the yarn through the original stitch to form a loop. This loop is the new stitch.

3 Slip the original stitch off the left-hand needle by gently pulling the right-hand needle to the right. Repeat these steps till you have knitted all the stitches on the left-hand needle. To work the next row, transfer the needle with all the stitches into your left hand.

Purl stitch

As with knit stitch, purl stitch can be formed in two ways. If you are new to knitting, try both techniques to see which works better for you: left-handed people may find the Continental method easier to master.

US/UK style

1 Hold the needle with the stitches in your left hand, and then insert the point of the right-hand needle into the front of the first stitch from right to left. Wind the yarn around the point of the right-hand needle, from right to left.

2 With the tip of the right-hand needle, pull the yarn through the stitch to form a loop. This loop is the new stitch.

3 Slip the original stitch off the left-hand needle by gently pulling the right-hand needle to the right. Repeat these steps till you have purled all the stitches on the left-hand needle. To work the next row, transfer the needle with all the stitches into your left hand.

Continental style

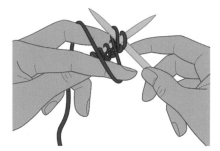

1 Hold the needle with the stitches to be knitted in your left hand, and then insert the tip of the right-hand needle into the front of the first stitch from right to left. Holding the yarn fairly taut at the front of the work, move the tip of the right-hand needle under the working yarn, then push your left index finger downwards, as shown, to hold the yarn around the needle.

2 With the tip of the right-hand needle, bring the yarn through the original stitch to form a loop.

3 Slip the original stitch off the left-hand needle by gently pulling the right-hand needle to the right. Repeat these steps till you have purled all the stitches on the left-hand needle. To work the next row, transfer the needle with all the stitches into your left hand.

Binding (casting) off

You need to bind (cast) off the stitches to complete the projects and stop the knitting unraveling.

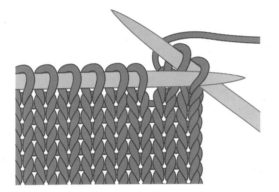

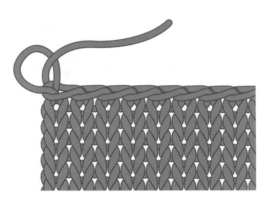

1 First knit two stitches in the normal way. With the point of the left-hand needle, pick up the first stitch you have just knitted and lift it over the second stitch. Knit another stitch so that there are two stitches on the right-hand needle again. Repeat the process of lifting the first stitch over the second stitch. Continue this process until there is just one stitch remaining on the right-hand needle.

2 Break the yarn, leaving a tail of yarn long enough to sew the work together (see page 124). Pull the tail all the way through the last stitch. Slip the stitch off the needle and pull it fairly tightly to make sure it is secure.

Slipping stitches

This means moving stitches from one needle to the other without knitting or purling them. They can be slipped knitwise or purlwise depending on the row you are working, or any specific pattern instructions.

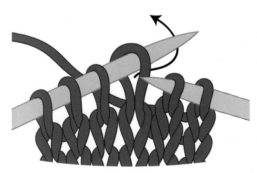

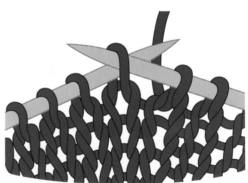

Knitwise
From left to right, put the right-hand needle into the next stitch on the left-hand needle (as shown by the arrow) and slip it across onto the right-hand needle without working it.

Purlwise
You can slip a stitch purlwise on a purl row or a knit row. From right to left, put the right-hand needle into the next stitch on the left-hand needle and slip it across onto the right-hand needle without working it.

Knitted fabrics

Only simple combinations of knit and purl stitches are used for most of the projects in this book.

Stockinette (stocking) stitch

To make this stitch, work alternate rows of knit and purl stitches. The front of the fabric is the side facing you as you work the knit rows. This stitch is used for the main part of most of the projects.

Garter stitch

To make this very simple stitch, you simply knit every row.

Seed (moss) stitch

To make this textured stitch, you knit 1 stitch then purl 1 stitch across a row. On the next row you knit the stitches that were knitted and purl the stitches that were purled on the previous row.

Single rib

To make this stitch, you knit 1 stitch then purl 1 stitch across a row. On the next row you purl the stitches that were knitted and vice versa to make the columns of this very stretchy fabric.

Double rib

This is made using the same principles as single rib, but two consecutive stitches are knitted or purled across each row.

Picking up stitches

For some projects, you will need to pick up stitches along either a horizontal edge (the cast-on or bound-/cast-off edge of your knitting), or a vertical edge (the edges of your rows of knitting).

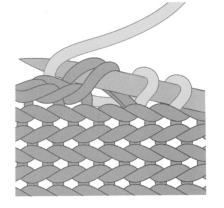

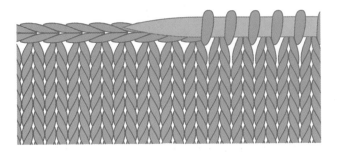

Along a row-end edge

With the right side of the knitting facing you, insert a knitting needle from the front to back between the first and second stitches of the first row. Wind the yarn around the needle and pull through a loop to form the new stitch. Normally you have more gaps between rows than stitches you need to pick up and knit. To make sure your picking up is even, you will have to miss a gap every few rows.

Along a cast-on or bound- (cast-) off edge

This is worked in the same way as picking up stitches along a vertical edge, except that you will work through the cast-on stitches rather than the gaps between rows. You will normally have the same number of stitches to pick up and knit as there are existing stitches.

Yarnover (yo)

To make a yarnover you wind the yarn around the right-hand needle to make an extra loop that is worked as a stitch on the next row. Winding the yarn around twice creates a double yarnover (yo twice).

Bring the yarn between the tips of the needles to the front. Take the yarn over the right-hand needle to the back and knit the next stitch on the left-hand needle (see page 114).

Be sure not to confuse "yo" with the abbreviations "yf" or "yb", both of which are used in this book (see page 126 for explanations of these terms).

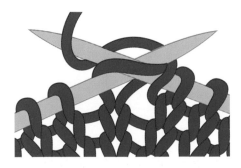

Increasing

There are three methods of increasing used in projects in this book.

Increase on a knit row (inc)

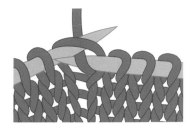
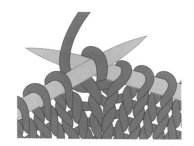
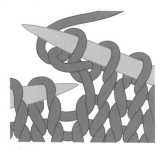

1 Knit the next stitch on the left-hand needle in the usual way (see page 114), but do not slip the "old" stitch off the left-hand needle.

2 Move the right-hand needle behind the left-hand needle and put it into the same stitch again, but through the back of the stitch this time. Knit the stitch again.

3 Now slip the "old" stitch off the left-hand needle in the usual way.

Increase on a purl row (inc pwise)

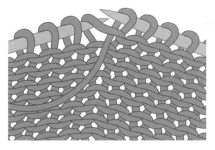
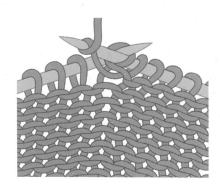

1 Purl the next stitch on the left-hand needle in the usual way (see page 115), but do not slip the "old" stitch off the left-hand needle.

2 Twist the right-hand needle backward to make it easier to put it into the same stitch again, but through the back of the stitch this time. Purl the stitch again, then slip the "old" stitch off the left-hand needle in the usual way.

Make one stitch (m1)

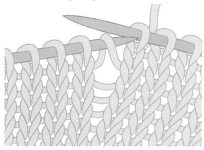
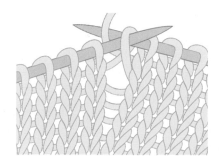

1 From the front, slip the tip of the left-hand needle under the horizontal strand of yarn running between the last stitch on the right-hand needle and the first stitch on the left-hand needle.

2 Put the right-hand needle knitwise into the back of the loop formed by the picked-up strand and knit into it in the normal way. (It is important to knit into the back of the loop so that it is twisted and a hole does not form in your work.)

Decreasing

There are five different ways of decreasing used in this book, one of which decreases by two stitches rather than one stitch.

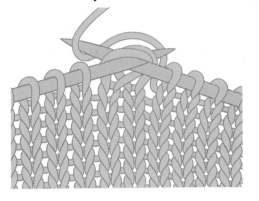

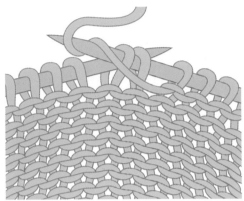

Knit two together (k2tog)

This is the simplest way of decreasing. Simply insert the right-hand needle through two stitches instead of the normal one, and then knit them in the usual way. The same principle is used to knit three stitches together; just insert the right-hand needle through three instead of through two.

Purl two together (p2tog)

To make a simple decrease on a purl row, insert the right-hand needle through two stitches instead of the normal one, and then purl them in the usual way.

Slip one, knit one, pass the slipped stitch over (skpo)

Slip the first stitch knitwise from the left-hand to the right-hand needle without knitting it. Knit the next stitch. Then lift the slipped stitch over the knitted stitch and drop it off the needle.

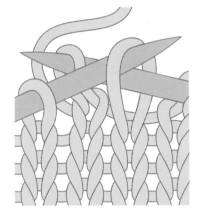

Slip, slip, knit (ssk)

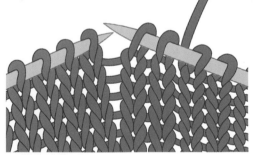

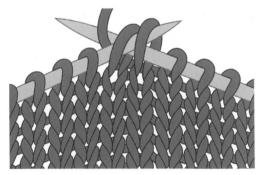

1 Slip one stitch knitwise, and then the next stitch knitwise onto the right-hand needle, without knitting them.

2 Insert the left-hand needle from left to right through the front loops of both the slipped stitches and knit them in the usual way.

Slip one, knit two together, pass the slipped stitch over (sk2po)
Reduce the number of stitches by two using this decrease.

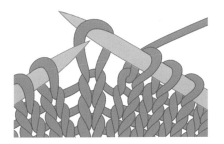 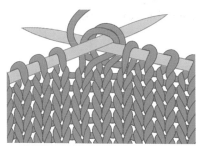 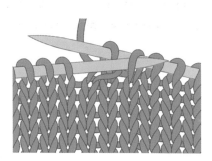

1 Slip the first stitch knitwise from the left-hand to the right-hand needle (see page 116).

2 Knit the next two stitches on the left-hand needle together (see page 120).

3 Lift the slipped stitch over the knitted stitch and drop it off the right-hand needle.

Crochet chain

While the projects in this book are all knitted rather than crocheted, a few of them require a simple crochet chain.

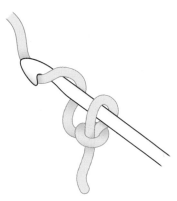 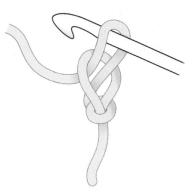

1 Make a slip knot on the crochet hook in the same way as for knitting (see page 113). Holding the slip stitch on the hook, wind the yarn around the hook from the back to the front, then catch the yarn in the crochet-hook tip.

2 Pull the yarn through the slip stitch on the crochet hook to make the second link in the chain. Continue in this way till the chain is the length needed.

Knitting in different colors

It's important to change colors in the right way to keep the knitted fabric flat and smooth and without any holes or gaps.

Stranding

If you are knitting just a few stitches in a different color, you can simply leave the color you are not using on the wrong side of the work and pick it up again when you need to.

Changing color on a knit row

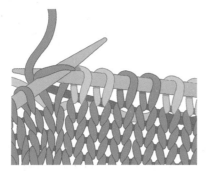

1 Knit the stitches (see page 114) in color A (brown in this example), bringing the yarn across over the strand of color B (lime in this example) to wrap around the needle.

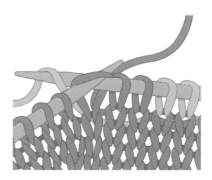

2 At the color change, drop color A and pick up color B, bringing it across under the strand of color A to wrap around the needle. Be careful not to pull it too tight. Knit the stitches in color B. When you change back to color A, bring it across over the strand of color B.

Changing color on a purl row

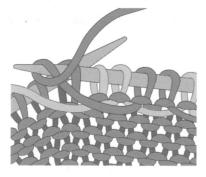

1 Purl the stitches (see page 115) in color A (brown in this example), bringing it across over the strand of color B (lime in this example) to wrap around the needle.

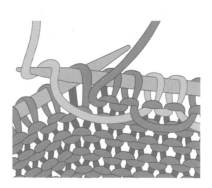

2 At the color change, drop color A and pick up color B, bringing it across under the strand of color A to wrap around the needle. Be careful not to pull it too tight. Purl the stitches in color B. When you change back to color A, bring it across over the strand of color B.

Intarsia

If you are knitting blocks of different colors within a project then you will need to use a technique called intarsia. This involves having separate balls of yarn for each area and twisting the yarns together where they join to avoid creating a hole or gap.

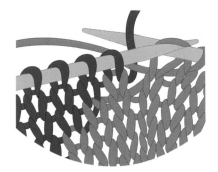
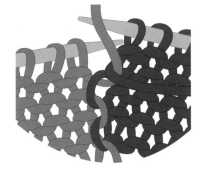
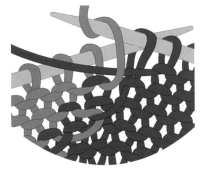

On the right side

When you want to change colors and the color change is vertical or sloping to the right, take the first color over the second color. Then pick up the second color, so the strands of yarn cross each other.

On the wrong side

On this side it is easy to see how the yarns must be interlinked at each color change.

This is worked in almost the same way as on the right side. When you want to change colors and the color change is vertical or sloping to the left, take the first color over the second color. Then pick up the second color, so the strands of yarn cross each other.

Embroidery stitches

The animals' features are embroidered using knitting yarn. When embroidering on knitting, take the embroidery needle in and out of the work between the strands that make up the yarn rather than between the knitted stitches themselves; this will help make your embroidery look more even.

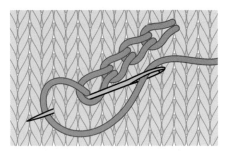

Chain stitch

Bring the yarn out at the starting point on the front of the work. Take your needle back into your knitting just next to the starting point, leaving a loop of yarn. Bring your needle out of the work again, a stitch length further on and catch in the loop. Pull the thread up firmly, but not so tight that it pulls the knitting. Continue in this way till the line, coil, or circle is complete.

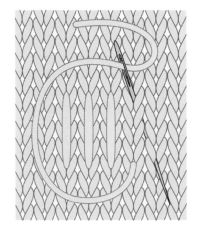

Straight stitch

To make this stitch, simply take the yarn out at the starting point and back down into the work where you want the stitch to end.

French knot

1 Bring the yarn out at the starting point, where you want the French knot to sit. Wind the yarn around your needle the required number of times.

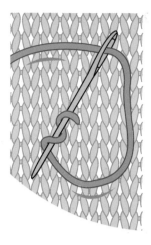

2 Take the needle back into the work, just to the side of the starting point. Then bring your needle out at the point for the next French knot or, if you are working the last or a single knot, to the back of your work. Continue pulling your needle through the work and slide the knot off the needle and onto the knitting.

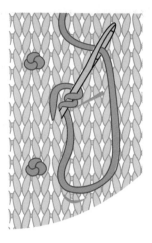

Sewing seams

There are various sewing-up stitches, and the patterns advise you on which method to use.

Mattress stitch on row-end edges

1 Right-sides up, lay the edges to be joined side by side. Thread a yarn sewing needle and from the back, bring it up between the first and second stitches of the left-hand piece, immediately above the cast-on edge. Take it across to the right-hand piece, and from the back bring it through between the first two stitches, immediately above the cast-on edge. Take it back to the left-hand piece and from the back, bring it through where it first came out. Pull the yarn through and this figure-of-eight will hold the cast-on edges level. Take the needle across to the right-hand piece and, from the front, take it under the bars of yarn between the first and second stitches on the next two rows up.

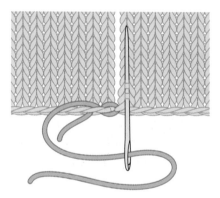

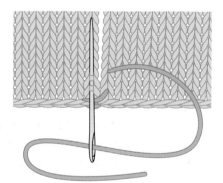

2 Take the needle across to the left-hand piece and, from the front, take it under the bars of yarn between the first and second stitches on the next two rows up. Continue in this way, taking the needle under two bars on one piece and then the other, to sew up the seam.

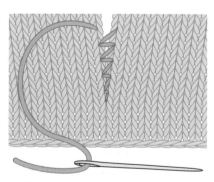

3 When you have sewn about 1in (2.5cm), gently and evenly pull the stitches tight to close the seam, and then continue to complete the sewing.

Mattress stitch on cast-on and bound- (cast-) off edges

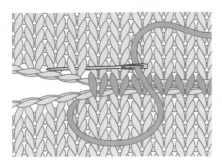

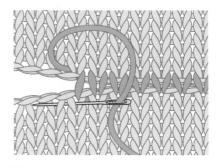

1 Right-sides up, lay the two edges to be joined side by side. Thread a yarn sewing needle with a tail left after binding (casting) off, or a long length of yarn.

Secure the yarn on the back of the lower knitted piece, then bring the needle up through the middle of the first whole stitch in that piece. Take the needle under both "legs" of the first whole stitch on the upper piece, so that it comes to the front between the first and second stitches.

2 Go back into the lower piece and take the needle through to the back where it first came out, and then bring it back to the front in the middle of the next stitch along. Pull the yarn through. Take the needle under both "legs" of the next whole stitch on the upper piece. Repeat this step to sew the seam. Pull the stitches gently taut to close the seam as you work.

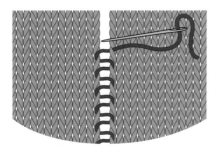

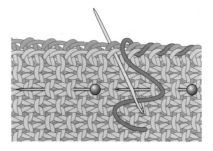

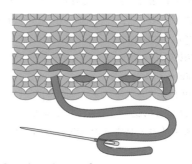

Flat stitch

This stitch creates a join that is completely flat.

Right-sides up, lay the two edges to be joined side by side. Thread a yarn sewing needle with a tail left after binding (casting) off, or a long length of yarn. Pick up the very outermost strand of knitting from one piece and then the same strand on the other piece. Work your way along the seam, pulling the yarn up firmly every few stitches to close the seam.

Oversewing

This stitch can be worked with the right or the wrong sides of the work together. Thread a yarn sewing needle with a tail left after binding (casting) off, or a long length of yarn. Bring the yarn from the back of the work, over the edge of the knitting, and out through to the back again a short distance further on.

Sewing in ends

The easiest way to finish yarn ends is to run a few small stitches forward then backward through your work, ideally in a seam. It is a good idea to use a yarn sewing needle to do this and take the tail between the strands that make up your yarn, as this will help make sure the end stays in place.

abbreviations

approx.	approximately
beg	begin(ning)
cm	centimeter(s)
cont	continue
g	gram(s)
in	inch(es)
inc	increase on a knit row, by working into front and back of next stitch: see page 119
inc pwise	increase on a purl row, by working into front and back of next stitch: see page 119
k	knit
k2tog	knit two stitches together: see page 120
k3tog	knit three stitches together: see page 120
kwise	knitwise
m1	make one stitch, by knitting into the strand between two stitches: see page 119
m	meter(s)
mm	millimeter
oz	ounces
p	purl
p2tog	purl two stitches together, see page 120
psso	pass slipped stitch over, pass a slipped stitch over another stitch
p2sso	pass two slipped stitches over, pass two slipped stitches over another stitch
pwise	purlwise
rem	remain(ing)
rep	repeat
RS	right side

skpo	slip one stitch, knit one stitch, pass slipped stitch over knitted one, to decrease: see page 120
sk2po	slip one stitch, knit two stitches together, pass slipped stitch over stitches knitted together, to decrease: see page 121
sl1(2)	slip one (two) stitch(es), from the left-hand needle to the right-hand needle without knitting it (them): see page 116
ssk	slip one stitch, slip one stitch, knit slipped stitches together, to decrease: see page 120
st(s)	stitch(es)
st st	stockinette (stocking) stitch
WS	wrong side
WT	with yarn at back, slip next stitch pwise from left-hand to right-hand needle. Bring yarn forward between needles. Slip stitch from the right-hand needle back to left-hand needle. Take yarn back between needles. Turn work.
yb	yarn back, between the tips of the needles
yd	yard(s)
yf	yarn forward, between the tips of the needles
yo	yarnover, wrap yarn around needle between stitches, to increase and to make an eyelet: see page 118
yo twice	yarnover twice, wrap yarn twice around needle between stitches, to make an eyelet
[ ]	work instructions within square brackets as directed
*	work instructions after/between asterisk(s) as directed

author acknowledgments

I would like to thank Cindy Richards, Penny Craig, Sally Powell, Fahema Khanam, and everyone at CICO Books for coming up with the idea for this book, and for being such nice people to work with. I'd also like to thank my editor Kate Haxell, pattern checker Marilyn Wilson, photographer Penny Wincer, and stylist Nel Haynes for all their hard work. I'd like to thank my husband, Roger, and son, Louis, for their patience and positive criticism, and my sister, Louise, for being my yarn shopping buddy. Finally, I'd like to thank my parents, Paddy and David Goble, for loving what I do even though I trained to do something completely different.

suppliers

This is a list of some of the major suppliers of the yarns used in this book. For reasons of space, we cannot cover all stockists so please explore the local knitting shops and online stores in your own country. Please remember that from time to time companies will change the brands they supply or stock and will not always offer the full range. If you cannot find a particular yarn locally, there will usually be an excellent alternative and your local yarn store is the best place to ask about this.

USA

Knitting Fever Inc.
www.knittingfever.com
Stockist locator on website
Debbie Bliss, Katia, Sirdar, Sublime

Westminster Fibers
www.westminsterfibers.com
Stockist locator on website
James C Brett

King Cole
www.kingcole.com
Stockist locator on website

Jo-Ann Fabric and Craft Stores
Retail stores and online
www.joann.com
Stockist locator on website
Lion Brand, Patons

Lion Brand Yarns
Online store for Lion Brand yarns
Tel: +800 258 YARN (9276)
www.lionbrand.com
Stockist locator on website (USA, Mexico & Canada)

WEBS
www.yarn.com
Schachenmayr, Sirdar, Sublime

Canada
Diamond Yarn
Tel: +1 416 736 6111
www.diamondyarn.com
Stockist locator on website
Debbie Bliss, Hayfield, Katia, Sirdar, Sublime

UK

Love Knitting
www.loveknitting.com
Online sales
Bergere de France, Cascade, Hayfield, Katia, King Cole, Patons, Rowan, Schachenmayr, Sirdar, Sublime

John Lewis
Retail stores and online
Tel: 03456 049049
www.johnlewis.com
Telephone numbers of stores on website
Debbie Bliss, Patons, Rowan, Sirdar, Sublime, Wendy

Laughing Hens
Online store only
Tel: +44 (0) 1829 740903
www.laughinghens.com
Bergere de France, Debbie Bliss, King Cole, Patons, Rowan, Sublime, Wendy

Australia
Black Sheep Wool 'n' Wares
Retail store and online
Tel: +61 (0)2 6779 1196
www.blacksheepwool.com.au
Debbie Bliss, King Cole, Katia, Patons, Sirdar, Sublime, Wendy

Sun Spun
Retail store only (Canterbury, Victoria)
Tel: +61 (0)3 9830 1609
Debbie Bliss, Rowan, Sublime

Texyarns International PTY Ltd
Tel: +61 (0)3 9427 9009
www.texyarns.com
Stockist locator on website
Katia

Finding a yarn stockist in your country
The following websites will help you find stockists for these yarn brands in your country. Please note that not all brands or types of yarn will be available in all countries.

Bergere de France
www.bergeredefrance.com
Stockist locator and online sales

Cascade Yarns
www.cascadeyarns.com
Stockist locator on website

DROPS Design
www.garnstudio.com

Katia Yarns
Tel: +34 93 828 38 19
www.katia.com

Rowan Yarns
Tel: +44 (0) 1484 681881
www.knitrowan.com

Sirdar (inc. Hayfield & Sublime)
Tel: +44 (0) 1924 231682
www.sirdar.co.uk

index